Scoreboost®

Mathematics

ALGEBRAIC REASONING

Includes
FREE
Online
Practice!

New Readers Press®
ProLiteracy's publishing division

CONTENTS

Scoreboost® for the GED® Test
Mathematics: Algebraic Reasoning
ISBN 978-1-56420-465-3

Copyright © 2013 New Readers Press
New Readers Press
ProLiteracy's Publishing Division
104 Marcellus Street, Syracuse, New York 13204
www.newreaderspress.com

All rights reserved. No part of this book may be reproduced or transmitted in any form or by any means, electronic or mechanical, including photocopying, recording, or by any information storage and retrieval system, without permission in writing from the publisher.

Printed in the United States of America
20

Proceeds from the sale of New Readers Press materials support professional development, training, and technical assistance programs of ProLiteracy that benefit local literacy programs in the U.S. and around the globe.

Scoreboost® Developer: Caren Van Slyke
Revision Developer: Words & Numbers
Editorial Director: Terrie Lipke
Design and Production Director: James Wallace
Technology Specialist: Maryellen Casey
Senior Designer: Carolyn Wallace

GED® is a registered trademark of the American Council on Education (ACE) and administered exclusively by GED Testing Service LLC under license. This material is not endorsed or approved by ACE or GED Testing Service.

TI-30XS image courtesy of Texas Instruments.

The GED® Mathematical Reasoning Test will be given on the computer. Many of the items will be multiple-choice questions. Other item types include fill-in-the-blank, drop-down menu, drag-and-drop, and hot spots.

Fill-in-the-blank questions will have an empty box where you will type in your answer. The answer could be a word, number, or equation. If you need mathematical symbols, you can click on | Æ Symbol | at the top of the screen.

Type your answer in the box. You may use numbers, a decimal point (.), and/or a negative sign (–) in your answer.

Sacramento Auto Parts asked its workers to donate to a local charity. Altogether, the company gathered $1,653. The average donation was $28.50. What equation would you use to find out how many workers donated to the charity?

$$1653 \div 28.50 = x$$

Drop-down menu items will offer you several answers to choose from in order to complete a statement or equation. Put your cursor on the "Select…" box to see the options. Click on the correct answer option.

A drag-and-drop item will require you to click on images, words, or numbers and drag them to the correct place. For instance, you may have to assemble an equation by dragging parts of it to the correct boxes.

What is the equation for the slope of line *AB* when point *A* is (1, 1) and *B* is (5, –4)?

Click on the numbers you want to select and drag them into the boxes.

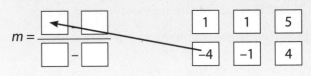

For a **hot spot** item, you will also drag an image to the correct place. In this way, you will plot a point on a grid, number line, or graph.

Ten people can sit at a round table at a party. There will be twice as many women as men.

$$2m + m \leq 10$$

Graph all possible solutions for *m*.

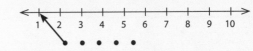

After you complete each Unit Review in this book, you can go to onlinepractice.newreaderspress.com to practice answering GED test questions in electronic format. If you'd like, you can complete this entire book and then go online and answer all the electronic Unit Review questions.

When you are finished with the online questions, you can print a score sheet. The score sheet includes a Scoreboost Action Plan to help you improve your score.

© New Readers Press. All rights reserved.

Add and Subtract Integers

You will be asked to add and subtract integers on the GED test. **Integers** include all whole numbers and their opposites. So, integers include positive and negative numbers.

These are the rules for adding integers:

- Always add two numbers at a time.
- If the numbers have the same sign, add them and keep the sign.
- If the numbers have different signs, subtract them and keep the sign of the number with the greater absolute value.

To subtract integers, change the problem to an addition problem, and then follow the addition rules. Subtracting a number is the same as adding its opposite.

Definition of Subtraction: $x - n = x + (-n)$

Every time you see a subtraction problem, change the operation to addition and then change the sign of the second number to its opposite.

Example

In one week, Caroline withdraws $45 from her account and deposits $123. What is the change in value for her account?

(A) −$168
(B) −$78
(C) $78
(D) $168

THINK: *I will add numbers with opposite signs.*

Step 1: Write the problem.
$$-45 + 123$$

Step 2: Because the signs are different, subtract the numbers. The answer will be positive because 123 is greater than 45.
$$-45 + 123 = 78$$

SOLUTION: (C) $78

GED Problem

Ben started his hike at 99 feet above sea level and ended it with a dive to 49 feet below sea level. What was his change in altitude in feet?

(A) −148
(B) −50
(C) 50
(D) 148

THINK: *I'll write the subtraction problem, and then change it to addition.*

Step 1: Write the problem. To find the change, start at his final height and subtract the initial height.
$$-49 - 99$$

Step 2: Change it to adding the opposite.
$$-49 + (-99)$$

Step 3: Simplify. The signs are the same. Add the numbers; keep the sign.
$$-49 + (-99) = -148$$

ANSWER: (A) −148

TESTWISE

When you subtract integers, remember to change the equation to adding the opposite. Then, you only have to remember the rules for adding integers.

© New Readers Press. All rights reserved.

Directions: Choose the correct answer for each problem. For problems 1–3, rewrite the problem as an addition problem.

1. 15 – (–3)

   (A) –18
   (B) –12
   (C) 12
   (D) 18

   Addition: _____

2. –22 – (–9)

   (A) –31
   (B) –13
   (C) 13
   (D) 31

   Addition: _____

3. –24 – 5

   (A) –29
   (B) –19
   (C) 19
   (D) 29

   Addition: _____

4. A football player gained 14 yards on a play. On the very next play, he lost three yards. What was his total yardage for those two plays?

   (A) –17
   (B) –11
   (C) 11
   (D) 17

5. Paul owes his mom $23. Reuben owes his mom $17. What is their total debt?

   (A) –$40
   (B) –$30
   (C) –$6
   (D) $16

6. At the end of the game, Fran had 14 points and Calvin had –22 points. By how many points did Fran win?

   (A) –36
   (B) –8
   (C) 8
   (D) 36

7. At noon the temperature was 22 degrees Fahrenheit. The low temperature that night was –4 degrees Fahrenheit. What was the change in temperature?

   (A) –26
   (B) –18
   (C) 17
   (D) 26

© New Readers Press. All rights reserved.

Answers start on page 45.

Multiply and Divide Integers

You will be asked to multiply and divide integers on the GED test.

These are the rules for multiplying integers:
- Always operate with two numbers at a time.
- If the numbers have the same sign, the answer is positive.
- If the numbers have different signs, the answer is negative.

That is, if you multiply two negative numbers, the answer is positive. If you multiply or divide a positive and a negative number, in either order, the answer is negative.

pos × pos = pos
pos × neg = neg
neg × pos = neg
neg × neg = pos

Dividing by a number is the same as multiplying by its reciprocal, so the same rules apply for division.

$x \div y = x \left(\frac{1}{y} \right)$

Example

Vern withdrew $12 from his savings account each week for 9 weeks. What was the total change in his balance?

- (A) −$108
- (B) −$21
- (C) $21
- (D) $108

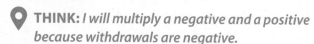 **THINK:** *I will multiply a negative and a positive because withdrawals are negative.*

Step 1: Write the problem.
  −12(9)

Step 2: The signs are different, so the answer is negative.
  −12(9) = −108

SOLUTION: (A) −$108

GED Problem

Dan owes $360 for his parking spot, but payment is divided evenly over 12 months. Which shows the correct way to write his monthly payment?

- (A) −$30
- (B) −$3
- (C) $3
- (D) $30

THINK: *I'll divide the total debt by 12.*

Step 1: Write the problem with debt as a negative number.
  −360 ÷ 12

Step 2: Simplify. The signs are different so the answer is negative.
  −360 ÷ 12 = −30

ANSWER: (A) −$30

TESTWISE

When you multiply more than two integers, multiply two integers at a time. Write the product, including the correct sign, and then multiply the product and the next integer. Continue until all factors have been multiplied.

© New Readers Press. All rights reserved.

Directions: Choose the correct answer for each problem. For problems 1–3, tell whether the signs are the same or different.

1. Parker gained 7 yards on each of three plays. What was his total yardage on those plays?

   (A) −21
   (B) −10
   (C) 10
   (D) 21

   Signs? _____

2. Nancy wrote a check for $325 each month for rent. What was the resulting change in her account over a year?

   (A) −$3,900
   (B) −$1,950
   (C) $1,950
   (D) $3,900

   Signs? _____

3. The temperature fell 42 degrees over 6 hours. What was the average change in temperature per hour?

   (A) −48
   (B) −7
   (C) 7
   (D) 48

   Signs? _____

4. $4(-14)$

   (A) −56
   (B) −18
   (C) 18
   (D) 56

5. $\dfrac{-56}{-8}$

   (A) −7
   (B) −6
   (C) 6
   (D) 7

6. $-12 \cdot -5$

   (A) −60
   (B) −17
   (C) 17
   (D) 60

7. $-1 \cdot -2 \cdot -3 \cdot 4$

   (A) −1,234
   (B) −144
   (C) −24
   (D) 24

© New Readers Press. All rights reserved.

Answers start on page 45.

Find Powers and Roots

Powers are a way to write repeated multiplication.

x^n means x multiplied by itself n times. The x is referred to as the **base,** and the n is the **exponent.** When a number is raised to the second power, or has an exponent of 2, we say the number is squared. When the exponent is 3, we say the number is cubed.

Here are some rules to use with powers.

- If two powers with the same base are multiplied, keep the base and add the exponents. $(x^n)(x^m) = x^{n+m}$

- If two powers with the same base are divided, keep the base and subtract the exponents. $\frac{x^n}{x^m} = x^{n-m}$

- If a power is raised to a power, keep the base and multiply the exponents. $(x^n)^m = x^{nm}$

Any number to the zero power equals 1. $x^0 = 1$.

If the base is negative, the result may be positive or negative. $-5^2 = -5 \cdot -5 = 25$ $-5^3 = -5 \cdot -5 \cdot -5 = -125$

When a base is inside parentheses, the entire value inside the parentheses is raised to the power. For example, $(-5)^2 = (-5) \cdot (-5) = 25$. Watch the placement of the parentheses: $-(5^2) = -(5 \cdot 5) \cdot -(25) = -25$.

A **root** is the opposite of a power. $\sqrt[n]{y}$ is called the nth root of y. It is the number that when multiplied by itself n times equals y. When n is 2, it is called a square root, and the 2 is not written outside the radical sign. When n is 3, it is called the cube root.

For every even root, there are two answers: one positive and one negative.

Example

What is $\frac{3^7}{3^5}$?

(A) 3
(B) 9
(C) 32
(D) 36

 **THINK:** *I can use exponent rules to simplify the powers.*

Step 1: Rewrite the powers.

$$\frac{3^7}{3^5} = 3^{7-5} = 3^2$$

Step 2: Simplify the powers.

$$3^2 = 9$$

SOLUTION: (B) 9

GED Problem

What is $\sqrt[4]{16} + 5^2$?

(A) 27
(B) 29
(C) 33
(D) 89

THINK: *I am looking for the number that when multiplied by itself 4 times equals 16.*

Step 1: Find the root.

$$\sqrt[4]{16} = 2 \text{ because } 2 \cdot 2 \cdot 2 \cdot 2 = 16.$$

Step 2: Find the power.

$$5^2 = 25$$

Step 3: Add the two numbers.

$$\sqrt[4]{16} + 5^2 = 2 + 25 = 27$$

ANSWER: (A) 27

TESTWISE

When using the exponent rules, be sure the bases of the powers are the same. If they are not the same, the rules do not apply.

© New Readers Press. All rights reserved.

Directions: Choose the correct answer for each problem. For problems 1–3, indicate whether the powers have the same base.

1. $3^2 \cdot 3^3$
   - (A) 15
   - (B) 18
   - (C) 243
   - (D) 729

   Same base? _____

2. $\dfrac{10^2}{5^2}$
   - (A) 0
   - (B) 1
   - (C) 2
   - (D) 4

   Same base? _____

3. $\dfrac{8^{16}}{8^{15}}$
   - (A) 1
   - (B) 8
   - (C) 9
   - (D) 16

   Same base? _____

4. $(2^2)^4$
   - (A) 16
   - (B) 64
   - (C) 128
   - (D) 256

5. -3^2
   - (A) −9
   - (B) −6
   - (C) 6
   - (D) 9

6. $\sqrt[5]{32}$
   - (A) 1
   - (B) 2
   - (C) 6.4
   - (D) 160

7. $\sqrt{121}$
   - (A) −11
   - (B) 11
   - (C) 11 and −11
   - (D) 242

8. $\sqrt[3]{-64}$
   - (A) −4
   - (B) −2
   - (C) 2
   - (D) 4

Answers start on page 45.

© New Readers Press. All rights reserved.

Evaluate Expressions

An algebraic expression is a series of operations written with numbers, operation signs, and variables. A **variable** is a letter, or symbol, that can represent different values. If you are given the values for the variables, you can **evaluate,** or find the value of, the expression. When asked to evaluate an expression, you should substitute the given values of the variables into the expression and simplify the expression. In other words, you find the value of the expression after you've exchanged each variable for its given value.

To simplify an expression, you must follow the **order of operations:**
1. Work within parentheses or other grouping symbols
2. Simplify powers and roots
3. Multiply or divide from left to right
4. Add or subtract from left to right

The fraction or division bar acts like a grouping symbol. It is as if the numerator is in parentheses and the denominator is in parentheses. So, first you simplify the numerator, then simplify the denominator, and last you divide.

Example

Evaluate $d - bt$ for $d = -10$, $b = 3$, and $t = -4$.

   (A) −22
   (B) 2
   (C) 22
   (D) 52

 THINK: *I can substitute values for variables, and then simplify the expression.*

Step 1: Substitute.
$$d - bt = -10 - 3(-4)$$

Step 2: Simplify using the order of operations.
$$= -10 - 3(-4) \quad \text{Multiply.}$$
$$= -10 + 12 \quad \text{Add.}$$
$$= 2$$

SOLUTION: (B) 2

GED Problem

Evaluate $\dfrac{fg}{f+h}$ when $f = 6$, $g = 5$, and $h = 4$.

   (A) 3
   (B) 6.5
   (C) 9
   (D) 13.5

 **THINK:** *I can substitute and simplify.*

Step 1: Substitute.
$$\frac{fg}{f+h} = \frac{6(5)}{6+4}$$

Step 2: Simplify.
$$\frac{6(5)}{6+4} = \frac{30}{10} = 3$$

Multiply on top. Add on bottom. Then, divide.

ANSWER: (A) 3

TESTWISE

There is a difference between -4^2 and $(-4)^2$. For -4^2, you square 4 and then multiply by −1, so $-4^2 = -16$. With $(-4)^2$, you multiply $(-4)(-4) = 16$. When the negative number is in parentheses, the negative number is raised to a power. When the negative number is not in parentheses, the number is raised to a power, and then the negative sign is applied to the result.

© New Readers Press. All rights reserved.

Directions: Choose the correct response for each problem. For problems 1–3, show your substitution.

1. Evaluate $-x^4$ when $x = 1$.

   (A) −4

   (B) −1

   (C) 1

   (D) 4

   After substitution: _____

2. Evaluate $ft - \dfrac{t}{z}$ when $f = -2$, $t = 12$, and $z = 3$.

   (A) −28

   (B) −12

   (C) 4

   (D) 20

   After substitution: _____

3. Evaluate $4 - 2x^3$ when $x = 3$.

   (A) −212

   (B) −50

   (C) 18

   (D) 54

   After substitution: _____

4. Evaluate $10 - 4d$ when $d = -3$.

   (A) −18

   (B) −2

   (C) 2

   (D) 22

5. Evaluate $2w + 5x$ when $w = -3$ and $x = -6$.

   (A) 50

   (B) −24

   (C) −36

   (D) −53

6. Evaluate $p + st$ when $p = -2$, $s = 4$, and $t = 5$.

   (A) 10

   (B) 12

   (C) 18

   (D) 22

7. Evaluate $\dfrac{m+n}{2(m-n)}$ when $m = 3$ and $n = 1$.

   (A) −4

   (B) −1

   (C) 1

   (D) 8

8. Evaluate $r(3x + 1)$ when $r = 12$ and $x = -3$.

   (A) −120

   (B) −96

   (C) 12

   (D) 384

© New Readers Press. All rights reserved.

Answers start on page 45.

Integer and Expression Strategies

Part I: You *may* use a calculator.
For questions 1–8, choose the one best answer.

1. Caroline deposits $340 into her account. Then she withdraws $115. What is the change in the balance on her account?

   (A) −$455
   (B) −$225
   (C) $225
   (D) $455

2. Evaluate $\frac{3n+8}{h}$ when $n = -6$ and $h = -2$.

   (A) −13
   (B) −10
   (C) −5
   (D) 5

3. Robert played a card game four times. Each time he lost 12 points. What was his total number of points?

   (A) −48
   (B) −3
   (C) 16
   (D) 48

4. Terry spent $10, $12, and $17. What was the average amount of money she spent?

   (A) −$13
   (B) −$22
   (C) −$29
   (D) −$39

5. What is $\sqrt[3]{-27}$?

   (A) −9
   (B) −3
   (C) 3
   (D) 9

6. Evaluate $\frac{-p^2}{q}$ when $p = 4$ and $q = 2$.

   (A) −8
   (B) −4
   (C) 4
   (D) 8

7. Henry dove to 104 feet below sea level. Then he climbed to 288 feet above sea level. What was the change in his height in feet?

   (A) −392
   (B) −184
   (C) 184
   (D) 392

8. $4^3 - 2^5$

   (A) 4
   (B) 16
   (C) 32
   (D) 64

© New Readers Press. All rights reserved.

Part II: You _may not_ use a calculator.
For questions 9–13, choose the one best answer.

9. Evaluate $4m^2 - 3$ when $m = -3$

    (A) −4
    (B) −2
    (C) 33
    (D) 141

10. Simplify: $2^2 \cdot 2^3$

    (A) 10
    (B) 24
    (C) 32
    (D) 1,024

11. Simplify: $\sqrt{144}$

    (A) 12 and −12
    (B) 12
    (C) −12
    (D) 72

12. Simplify: $\left(3^2\right)^2$

    (A) 12
    (B) 25
    (C) 36
    (D) 81

13. Evaluate $\dfrac{-2x^2}{z+b}$ when $x = -4$, $z = 11$, and $b = 5$.

    (A) −4
    (B) −2
    (C) 2
    (D) 4

14. Simplify: $-26 + 39$

    (A) −65
    (B) −13
    (C) 13
    (D) 65

15. Simplify: $12 - (-24)$

    (A) −36
    (B) −12
    (C) 12
    (D) 36

16. Simplify: $-2 \cdot -3 \cdot -4$

    (A) −24
    (B) −10
    (C) 20
    (D) 32

17. $-32 \div 8 =$

    (A) −24
    (B) −4
    (C) 4
    (D) 24

For more practice with answering questions like this on the computer, you can go to onlinepractice.newreaderspress.com.

SCOREBOOST ACTION PLAN

Check your answers starting on page 45. Fill in the chart, and make an action plan.

Results
0–9 correct • _Need to study more—make a plan_
10–13 correct • _Need to review some skills_
14–17 correct • _Mastery of skills—move on_

Questions	Strategy	Pages	Correct/Total	Plan: More work needed
1, 7, 14, 15	Add and Subtract Integers	4–5	_____ /4	☐
3, 4, 16, 17	Multiply and Divide Integers	6–7	_____ /4	☐
5, 8, 10, 11, 12	Powers and Roots	8–9	_____ /5	☐
2, 6, 9, 13	Expressions	10–11	_____ /4	☐
		Total:	_____ **/17**	

© New Readers Press. All rights reserved.

Write and Solve Equations

Some GED problems require you to write an **equation** and/or solve it.

Remember to solve an equation means to find the value of the variable that makes the number sentence true. To solve an equation, use inverse operations to isolate the variable on one side of the equation.

Example

The sum of two numbers is 48. The second number is 15 more than twice the first number. What is the first number?

(A) 8
(B) 11
(C) 15
(D) 37

 **THINK:** *I can use algebraic language to write an equation, and then solve it.*

Step 1: Write an expression for each number. The variable n represents the first number. The second number is 15 more than twice the first number.

Let n = the first number
Let $2n + 15$ = the second number

Step 2: Write an equation showing that the sum of the numbers is 48.

$n + 2n + 15 = 48$

Step 3: Solve the equation.

$$n + 2n + 15 = 48$$
$$3n + 15 = 48$$
$$3n = 33$$
$$n = 11$$

SOLUTION: (B) 11 is the first number.

GED Problem

Pablo weighs 20 pounds more than Keeley, and Jasmine weighs 30 pounds less than twice as much as Keeley. If Pablo and Jasmine weigh the same, how much does Keeley weigh?

(A) 50 pounds
(B) 60 pounds
(C) 70 pounds
(D) 80 pounds

 **THINK:** *I can use algebraic language to write an equation and solve it.*

Step 1: Write an expression for each person's weight.

Let n = Keeley's weight
Let $n + 20$ = Pablo's weight
Let $2n - 30$ = Jasmine's weight

Step 2: Write an equation to show that Pablo and Jasmine weigh the same.

$n + 20 = 2n - 30$

Step 3: Solve the equation.

$$n + 20 = 2n - 30$$
$$n + 50 = 2n$$
$$50 = n$$

ANSWER: (A) 50 pounds

TESTWISE

Look at the question when you are trying to define the variable. What is it asking for? Often what the question is asking for is the definition of the variable.

© New Readers Press. All rights reserved.

Directions: Choose the answer for each problem. For problems 1–3, first decide what unknown quantity the variable will represent.

1. Ally went on a 3-day driving trip. On the 2nd day, she drove 100 miles less than twice the distance she drove on the 1st day. On the 3rd day, she drove twice the distance she drove on the 2nd day. If she drove 500 miles on the 3rd day, how far did she drive on the first day?

   (A) 175
   (B) 250
   (C) 325
   (D) 550

   Let $x = $ _____

2. One more than a number is the same as 5 times a number decreased by 15. What is the number?

   (A) 2
   (B) 4
   (C) 5
   (D) 8

   Let $n = $ _____

3. Bill earns $40 more than half Rita's weekly pay. If their combined pay for a week is $520, how much does Rita earn weekly?

   (A) $220
   (B) $260
   (C) $320
   (D) $480

   Let $p = $ _____

4. Ned has 55 marbles in his collection. He has twice as many white marbles as red marbles. He has five more blue marbles than white marbles. How many white marbles does Ned have?

   (A) 5
   (B) 10
   (C) 11
   (D) 20

5. Maggie is four times as old as her cousin Samuel. In five years, she will be six years less than three times his age. How old is Samuel now?

   (A) 4
   (B) 9
   (C) 16
   (D) 21

6. One number is equal to the product of –2 and the difference between another number (n) and 5. The sum of the numbers is 16. What is the second number?

   (A) –22
   (B) –6
   (C) 6
   (D) 22

Answers start on page 45.

© New Readers Press. All rights reserved.

Evaluate Functions

A **function** is a special relation for which one value depends on the other. Each input gives exactly one output.

A function is often written as an equation. There is only one possible output, *y,* when you substitute for an input, *x,* in a function. Functions are used to model real-life experiences.

Example

An employee is paid by the hour. She earns $9.50 for each hour she works. How much will she earn in 30 hours?

   (A) $39.50
   (B) $275
   (C) $285
   (D) $310.50

 THINK: *I can write and evaluate a function.*

Step 1: Write a function.

Let *h* be the number of hours she works and *P* be how much she is paid.

$P = 9.5h$

Step 2: Substitute 30 for *h* and evaluate the function.

$P = 9.5(30) = 285$

SOLUTION: (C) She will earn $285.

GED Problem

Renting a video arcade for a birthday party costs $200 plus $8 per guest. How much will a party cost if there are 13 guests?

   (A) $104
   (B) $213
   (C) $304
   (D) $2,608

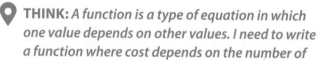 **THINK:** *A function is a type of equation in which one value depends on other values. I need to write a function where cost depends on the number of guests, and then substitute to find the function's value for 13 guests.*

Step 1: Renting the arcade costs $200 plus $8 per guest. If *x* is the number of guests, 8*x* is the fee for the guests. If I add 200 to that amount, I get the total cost. One way to write the function is: $C = 8x + 200$.

Step 2: Evaluate the function for $x = 13$.

$C = 8(13) + 200$
$C = 104 + 200$
$C = 304$

ANSWER: (C) $304

TESTWISE

Word problems sometimes require us to write a function to model a situation. A function describes the way two quantities are related, so check to be sure the function you use is true for every value of the variable.

© New Readers Press. All rights reserved.

Directions: Choose the one correct answer for each problem. For problems 1–3, first decide what the function is.

1. Carly drove cross-country on vacation. Her average speed was 56 miles per hour. How far did she go in 24 hours?

   (A) 80 miles
   (B) 624 miles
   (C) 1,080 miles
   (D) 1,344 miles

   Function: _____

2. An annual membership at a swim club costs $30. Members must also pay a $5 monthly locker fee and a $2 fee each time they use the facility. What is the total annual cost for a member who uses the facility 81 times in one year? (*Hint:* There are 12 months in a year.)

   (A) $162
   (B) $192
   (C) $252
   (D) $597

   Function: _____

3. George is paid on commission. The amount he is paid depends on his sales. He earns 15% on all of his sales. How much does he make if his sales are $4,320?

   (A) $49.68
   (B) $648
   (C) $4,968
   (D) $64,800

   Function: _____

4. Marcus plans to open a checking account. His bank charges a monthly fee of $6 plus $0.10 per check for each check over ten written in the month. How much will Marcus pay in fees if he writes 17 checks one month?

   (A) $1.70
   (B) $5.30
   (C) $6.70
   (D) $103.70

5. In a family, the number of children invited to a birthday party depends on the birthday child's age. The child can invite two children for every year of his or her age. How many years old is the child who can invite 14 children to his birthday party?

   (A) 7
   (B) 14
   (C) 16
   (D) 28

6. There are approximately 2.54 centimeters in an inch. How many centimeters are there in a yard? (*Hint:* 1 yard = 36 inches)

   (A) 14.17
   (B) 30.48
   (C) 91.44
   (D) 182.88

Answers start on page 45.

© New Readers Press. All rights reserved.

Solve Inequalities

Writing and solving an inequality is a lot like writing and solving an equation.

An **inequality** expresses that two quantities are not equal by using the symbols:
- (≤) less than or equal to
- (<) less than
- (>) greater than
- (≥) greater than or equal to

Remember this rule when solving inequalities:
If you multiply or divide by a negative number, you must reverse the direction of the inequality symbol.

Example

Flora is paid $8 per hour for babysitting. She needs at least $208 to purchase a new desk. What is the smallest number of hours she must work?

(A) 20
(B) 25
(C) 26
(D) 30

 THINK: *I can write and solve an inequality.*

Step 1: Write an inequality.
Let h be the number of hours she works.

$$8h \geq 208$$

Step 2: Solve the inequality.

$$8h \geq 208$$
$$h \geq 26$$

SOLUTION: (C) She must work at least 26 hours.

GED Problem 1

Solve the inequality. $-3x + 15 < 45$

(A) $x > 10$
(B) $x > -10$
(C) $x < 10$
(D) $x < -10$

Step 1: Solve the inequality.

$$-3x + 15 < 45$$
$$-3x < 30$$
$$x > -10$$

Note that the inequality symbol changed direction because in the process of solving the inequality, you divided by –3.

Step 2: Write the solution. $x > -10$

ANSWER: (B) $x > -10$

GED Problem 2

Georgia has $64. She wants to buy flower bouquets for $12.50. Which inequality shows how many bouquets, b, she could buy?

(A) $b \leq 5$
(B) $b \geq 6$
(C) $b < 51.5$
(D) $b > 12.5$

 **THINK:** *Georgia can spend, at most, $64; I need to write an inequality.*

Step 1: Write an inequality.

$$12.5b \leq 64$$

Step 2: Solve the inequality.
$$\frac{12.5b}{12.5} \leq \frac{64}{12.5}$$
$$b \leq 5.12$$

Since you cannot buy a partial bouquet, she can buy at most 5 bouquets.

ANSWER: (A) $b \leq 5$

© New Readers Press. All rights reserved.

Directions: Choose the one correct answer for each problem. For problems 1–3, first write the inequality.

1. To join a dance class, there is an enrollment fee of $50 plus a monthly fee of $65. How many months of dance, *d*, can Audra take if she has $850 to spend on dance?

   (A) $d \leq 850$
   (B) $d \leq 17$
   (C) $d > 13$
   (D) $d \leq 12$

   Inequality: _____

2. Hope has $900 in her checking account. She has $76 per month that she must pay in bills. At most, how many months, *m*, can she pay all of her bills without making any additional deposits?

   (A) $m \leq 11$
   (B) $m \leq 12$
   (C) $m > 12$
   (D) $m \geq 11$

   Inequality: _____

3. Calvin makes 7% commission on his sales. How much must his sales, *s*, be if he wants to purchase a gaming system that costs $400?

   (A) $s \leq \$4,007.33$
   (B) $s \leq \$5,715.92$
   (C) $s \geq \$5,714.29$
   (D) $s > \$4,629.45$

   Inequality: _____

4. Frankie drives at most 65 miles per hour for 5 hours. If *m* is the number of miles Frankie has traveled, which inequality is true?

   (A) $m < 325$
   (B) $m \leq 325$
   (C) $m > 325$
   (D) $m \geq 325$

5. Emilien has four more tennis rackets than James. If together they have at least 18 rackets, how many rackets does James have (*j*)?

   (A) $j \leq 7$
   (B) $j \geq 7$
   (C) $j \leq 11$
   (D) $j \geq 11$

6. During the fall, the difference between the low and the high temperature each day averages 25 degrees. What must the low temperature, *t*, be for the high temperature to be at least 60 degrees?

   (A) $t \geq 35$
   (B) $t \geq 45$
   (C) $t < 35$
   (D) $t \leq 8$

TESTWISE

The phrases *at least* and *at most* can be confusing. Be sure to think about what they mean. *At least* means *that amount or more*, so you'll use greater than or equal to. *At most* means *that amount or less*, so you'll use less than or equal to.

Answers start on page 45.

© New Readers Press. All rights reserved.

Use FOIL with Quadratic Equations

Quadratic equations are equations in which the greatest power of the variable is 2. In standard form, a quadratic equation looks like $y = ax^2 + bx + c$. When you solve quadratic equations, y must equal 0.

When you multiply two binomials, use the **FOIL** method. FOIL stands for **F**irst, **O**uter, **I**nner, **L**ast. Multiply these pairs of terms in order to find the product.

Combine like terms and you find that $(x + 2)(x - 4) = x^2 - 2x - 8$.

$$\text{Outer}$$
$$\text{First}$$
$$(x + 2)(x - 4) = x^2 - 4x + 2x - 8$$
$$\text{Inner}$$
$$\text{Last}$$

There are two ways to solve, or find the two solutions for, quadratic equations. The first is factoring, which is the opposite of FOIL. When you are given a quadratic equation in standard form, set the equation equal to 0. You can find the two numbers that multiply to give you c and add to give you b.

If you are told that $x^2 - x - 6 = 0$, then to factor, you find two numbers with a product of -6 and a sum of -1. Those numbers are -3 and 2 because $-3(2) = -6$ and $-3 + 2 = -1$. Therefore, you can write $x^2 - x - 6 = 0 = (x - 3)(x + 2)$.

Because you know by substitution that $(x - 3)(x + 2) = 0$, using the Zero Property of Multiplication tells you that either $(x - 3) = 0$ or $(x + 2) = 0$. After solving the equations, this means your two solutions are $x = 3$ and $x = -2$.

Example

Solve. $m^2 - 8m - 20 = 0$

    (A) $m = 10$ or -2
    (B) $m = 5$ or 4
    (C) $m = -10$ or 2
    (D) $m = -4$ or -5

THINK: *I can factor the equation.*

Step 1: Find two numbers with a product of -20 and a sum of -8: -10 and 2

Step 2: Solve $(m - 10)(m + 2) = 0$
If $m - 10 = 0$, $m = 10$.
If $m + 2 = 0$, then $m = -2$.

SOLUTION: (A) $m = 10$ or -2

The second method you can use to solve a quadratic equation is the quadratic formula. For $x^2 - x - 6 = 0$, $a = 1$, $b = -1$, and $c = -6$. Substitute these values into the quadratic formula to find the values of x.

$$x = \frac{-b \pm \sqrt{b^2 - 4ac}}{2a}$$

$$x = \frac{-(-1) \pm \sqrt{(-1)^2 - 4(1)(-6)}}{2(1)}$$

$$x = \frac{1 \pm \sqrt{25}}{2}$$

$$x = \frac{1 \pm 5}{2}$$

$$x = 3, -2$$

GED Problem

Solve $b^2 + 20b = 80$

    (A) $b = -7.76, -12.24$
    (B) $b = -23.42, 3.42$
    (C) $b = -12.25, -27.75$
    (D) $b = 7.32, -27.32$

THINK: *I can use the quadratic formula.*

Step 1: Set one side of the equation equal to 0:
$b^2 + 20b - 80 = 0$

Step 2: Identify a, b, and c: $a = 1$, $b = 20$, $c = -80$

Step 3: Substitute into the formula and solve. Round your answer to the nearest hundredth.

$$x = \frac{-b \pm \sqrt{b^2 - 4ac}}{2a}$$

$$x = \frac{-20 \pm \sqrt{20^2 - 4(1)(-80)}}{2(1)}$$

$$x = \frac{-20 \pm \sqrt{720}}{2}$$

$$x = -23.416, 3.416$$

ANSWER: (B) $b = -23.42, 3.42$

© New Readers Press. All rights reserved.

Directions: Choose the one correct answer for each problem. For problems 1–3, tell what the coefficients are in the equation. For problems 4–6, show the factors.

quadratic formula $\quad x = \dfrac{-b \pm \sqrt{b^2 - 4ac}}{2a}$

1. Solve using the quadratic formula. Round your answer to the nearest thousandth.

   $n^2 - 6n = 1$

   (A) $n = 1.622, -6.162$
   (B) $n = 6.162, -0.162$
   (C) $n = -8.268, -11.732$
   (D) $n = -9.487, 9.487$

   $a = $ _____ $\qquad b = $ _____ $\qquad c = $ _____

2. Solve using the quadratic formula.

   $2p^2 - 3p - 5 = 0$

   (A) $p = 1, \dfrac{5}{2}$

   (B) $p = 5, \dfrac{1}{2}$

   (C) $p = -1, \dfrac{5}{2}$

   (D) $p = -\dfrac{1}{2}, 5$

   $a = $ _____ $\qquad b = $ _____ $\qquad c = $ _____

3. Solve using the quadratic formula.

   $r^2 + 3r - 7 = 3$

   (A) $r = 3.083, -9.083$
   (B) $r = -3, 9$
   (C) $r = 2, -5$
   (D) $r = 9.124, -9.124$

   $a = $ _____ $\qquad b = $ _____ $\qquad c = $ _____

4. Solve by factoring.

   $k^2 + 6k = 16$

   (A) $k = 2, 8$
   (B) $k = -2, 8$
   (C) $k = -2, -8$
   (D) $k = 2, -8$

   Factors: _____

5. Solve by factoring.

   $d^2 + 16d + 55 = 0$

   (A) $d = -5, -11$
   (B) $d = 5, 11$
   (C) $d = -5, 11$
   (D) $d = 5, -11$

   Factors: _____

6. Solve by factoring.

   $y^2 - 7y = -10$

   (A) $y = 3, 4$
   (B) $y = -3, -4$
   (C) $y = -2, -5$
   (D) $y = 2, 5$

   Factors: _____

© New Readers Press. All rights reserved.

TESTWISE

Before you start to solve a quadratic equation, be sure that one side of the equation equals 0. Also, check your factoring by using the FOIL method. The result of the FOIL should be the original equation.

Answers start on page 45.

Fill-in-the-Blank Equations and Inequality Questions

Some GED problems require you type your answer into a box. These are called **fill-in-the-blank** problems.

When you have a fill-in-the-blank equation or inequality question, you work it just like you would a multiple choice problem. If necessary, translate the word problem to an equation, and then solve the equation or inequality. Then you will type your answer into a box rather than choosing from a list of possible answers.

Example

The second of two numbers is four times the first. Their sum is 65. What is the greater number?

The greater number is _____.

 THINK: *I can use algebraic language to write an equation, and then solve it.*

Step 1: Write expressions for each number. The variable *n* represents the first number. The second number is four times the first number.

Let n = the first number
Let $4n$ = the second number

Step 2: Write an equation showing the sum of the numbers is 65.

$n + 4n = 65$

Step 3: Solve the equation.

$n + 4n = 65$
$5n = 65$
$n = 13$

Step 4: Answer the question.
The question is "What is the greater number?"
The second number is four times the first.

$4n = 4(13) = 52$

SOLUTION: [52]

GED Problem

A soccer player shot at least 12 times in 1 game. The number of missed goals was eight more than the number of goals scored. How many goals did the player score?

The player scored at least _____ goals.

 THINK: *I can use algebraic language to write an inequality and solve it.*

Step 1: Write an expression for goals scored and missed goals.

Let g = goals scored
Let $g + 8$ = goals missed

Step 2: Write an inequality to show the number of shots taken.

$g + g + 8 \geq 12$

Step 3: Solve the inequality.

$g + g + 8 \geq 12$
$2g + 8 \geq 12$
$2g \geq 4$
$g \geq 2$

ANSWER: The player scored at least [2] goals.

© New Readers Press. All rights reserved.

TESTWISE

Before you type in your answer, be sure to reread the problem. Are you answering the correct question? Make sure you have addressed what the problem asked for. For example, you may solve an equation to find the value of a lesser number, but the question may ask for the greater number. You may need to use the lesser number to calculate the greater number.

Directions: Write your answer in the box. You may use numbers, a decimal point (.), and/or a negative sign (–) in your answer. For problems 1–6, first decide what unknown quantity the variable will represent.

1. The length of a tennis court is 78 feet. This is 3 less than 3 times the width of the court. What is the width of the court?

   Let $x =$ _____

   The width of the court is ☐ feet.

2. One number is –3 times the first number. The sum of the numbers is –4. What is the second number?

   Let $x =$ _____

   The second number is ☐ .

3. Tally earns $56 per day. This is at least $10 more per day than Frank earns.

   Let $x =$ _____

   Frank earns at most $ ☐ .

4. Hannah has 64 stamps in her collection. The number of new stamps is 11 less than 4 times the number of old stamps. How many new stamps does she have?

   Let $x =$ _____

   Hannah has ☐ new stamps.

5. Rad is 5 more than twice Brian's age in years. The sum of their ages is 35. How old is Rad?

   Let $x =$ _____

   Rad is ☐ years old.

6. In a 30-minute television show, the number of minutes of programming is six more than twice the number of minutes of advertisements. How many minutes of programming are there?

   Let $x =$ _____

   There are ☐ minutes of programming.

7. $-4x + 6 \leq 34$

   $x \geq$ ☐

8. $-30 = -9x + 6$

   $x =$ ☐

9. $-44 = -3x - 2$

   $x =$ ☐

10. $\frac{3}{4}x > 12$

    $x >$ ☐

Answers start on page 46.

© New Readers Press. All rights reserved.

Equations, Functions, and Inequalities

Part I: You *may* use a calculator.
For questions 1–4, choose the one best answer.
For questions 5 and 6, write your answer in the box.

quadratic formula $x = \dfrac{-b \pm \sqrt{b^2 - 4ac}}{2a}$

1. Solve using the quadratic formula.
   $x^2 - 10x - 7 = 3$

   (A) $x = 16.314, -6.314$
   (B) $x = 15.916, 4.084$
   (C) $x = -0.916, 10.916$
   (D) $x = 7.598, 2.042$

2. Solve. $-4x + 9 \leq 29$

   (A) $x \geq -5$
   (B) $x \leq -5$
   (C) $x > 9.5$
   (D) $x \leq -9.5$

3. The distance Yvonne is from home depends on the number of hours she has been driving. If Yvonne drives an average of 45 miles per hour, how many miles will she go in 3.5 hours?

   (A) 12.9
   (B) 41.5
   (C) 157.5
   (D) 180.3

4. The amount of money Jack earns depends on the number of yards he mows. Jack is paid $60 per yard. How much will he make if he mows seven yards?

   (A) $8.57
   (B) $67
   (C) $366
   (D) $420

5. It takes Bob twice as long as Caitlyn to clean his room. It takes Andrea ten minutes longer than Caitlyn to clean her room. In total, they work 90 minutes to clean their rooms. How long does it take Bob to clean his room?

   It takes Bob [ ] minutes to clean his room.

6. In the living room there are three times as many windows as in the dining room. The kitchen has four fewer windows than the dining room. There are 16 windows in the living room and the kitchen combined. How many windows are in the living room?

   There are [ ] windows in the living room.

© New Readers Press. All rights reserved.

Part II: You *may not* use a calculator.
For questions 7–10, choose the one best answer.
For questions 11 and 12, write your answers in the box.

7. Solve by factoring: $x^2 + 5x + 6 = 0$

   (A) $x = 2, 3$
   (B) $x = 1, 6$
   (C) $x = -1, 6$
   (D) $x = -2, -3$

8. Solve. $3x - 7 > -22$

   (A) $x > -5$
   (B) $x < 5$
   (C) $x < -\frac{29}{3}$
   (D) $x > \frac{25}{7}$

9. A square's perimeter depends on the length of one of its sides. The perimeter is four times the side length. If the perimeter is 28 meters, how long is each side?

   (A) 7 meters
   (B) 14 meters
   (C) 56 meters
   (D) 112 meters

10. Solve: $x^2 + 4x - 2 = 10$

    (A) $x = 6, -2$
    (B) $x = -6, 2$
    (C) $x = 4, -4$
    (D) $x = 4, 4$

11. Kenny wants to buy a new wakeboard for $360. He saves $22 per week from his paycheck. What is the smallest number of weeks he must save to be able to buy the wakeboard?

    He must save at least ☐ weeks.

12. The greater of two numbers is eight more than five times the lesser number. Their sum is 74. What is the greater number?

    The greater number is ☐.

For more practice with answering questions like this on the computer, you can go to onlinepractice.newreaderspress.com.

SCOREBOOST ACTION PLAN

Results
0–6 correct • *Need to study more—make a plan*
7–8 correct • *Need to review some skills*
9–12 correct • *Mastery of skills—move on*

Check your answers starting on page 46. Fill in the chart, and make an action plan.

Questions	Strategy	Pages	Correct/Total	Plan: More work needed
5, 6, 12	Equations	14–15	_____ /3	☐
3, 4, 9	Functions	16–17	_____ /3	☐
2, 8, 11	Inequalities	18–19	_____ /3	☐
1, 7, 10	Quadratic Equations	20–21	_____ /3	☐
		Total:	_____ /12	

© New Readers Press. All rights reserved.

Use Tables to Solve Algebra Problems

On the GED Math Test, an algebra word problem describes a situation in which you solve for an unknown. The unknown quantity is usually represented with a letter, such as x or n.

Constructing a **table** can help you organize your thinking and write an equation to represent the situation.

Example

John is six times as old as his little sister Anna. In twelve years, John will be twice as old as Anna. How old is John now?

	Anna's Age	**John's Age**
Now	x	$6x$
In 12 years	$x + 12$	$6x + 12$

$$6x + 12 = 2(x + 12)$$
$$6x + 12 = 2x + 24$$
$$4x = 12$$
$$x = 3$$

THINK: *I will create a table to make it easier to write an equation.*

Step 1: Let x represent Anna's age now. John is six times as old as Anna now, so let $6x$ represent John's age now. Add 12 to their current ages to express their ages in 12 years.

Step 2: Write an equation to represent the relationship between their ages in 12 years. In 12 years, John's age will be twice Anna's age, so the expression for John's age in 12 years equals twice the expression for Anna's age in 12 years. Solve for x.

Step 3: Now that you know the value of x, reread the problem to see what the question is asking. The problem asks you to find John's age now. Since Anna's age now is 3, John's age now is $6x = 6(3) = 18$.

SOLUTION: John is **18 years old** now.

GED Problem

A cashier has 90 dimes and nickels in his cash drawer. If the total value of the coins is $6.40, how many nickels are in the drawer?

(A) 26
(B) 38
(C) 52
(D) 63

THINK: *I will make a table to organize the information.*

Step 1: Let x = the number of nickels and $90 - x$ = the number of dimes. To work in whole numbers, express all of the values in cents.

	Nickels	**Dimes**
Number	x	$90 - x$
Value in cents	$5x$	$10(90 - x)$

Step 2: The total value of both types of coins equals $6.40 or 640 cents. Write and solve the equation.

$$5x + 10(90 - x) = 640$$
$$5x + 900 - 10x = 640$$
$$-5x = -260$$
$$5x = 260$$
$$x = 52$$

ANSWER: (C) 52

TESTWISE

As the example above shows, when you solve for x, you have not necessarily answered the question. Reread each problem to identify what the question is asking, and finish the solution if necessary.

© New Readers Press. All rights reserved.

Directions: Solve the problems below. For problems 1–3, first complete the table. For problems 4–6, you may make your own table.

1. Carrie is three times as old as David. In five years, Carrie will be only twice as old as David. How old will Carrie be in five years?

   (A) 20
   (B) 15
   (C) 10
   (D) 5

	David's Age	Carrie's Age
Now	x	
In 5 years		

2. The sum of four consecutive numbers is 230. What is the largest of these numbers? (*Hint:* Consecutive numbers are numbers in counting order; for example, 1, 2, 3.)

   (A) 56
   (B) 57
   (C) 59
   (D) 115

1st Number	2nd Number	3rd Number	4th Number
x	$x + 1$		

3. Donna earns twice as much money per month as Omar. Omar earns $200 more than Alex. Together, the three workers earn $3,320 per month. How much does Omar earn per month?

   (A) $680
   (B) $840
   (C) $880
   (D) $1,760

Alex	Omar	Donna
x		

4. A theater sold 300 tickets to a special benefit performance. The ticket prices were $4 for children and $6 for adults. If three times as many adults attended as children, how many adults attended?

   (A) 33
   (B) 75
   (C) 125
   (D) 225

5. Ryan drove 380 miles in 6 hours. He drove at an average rate of 70 miles per hour for the first part of the trip. He averaged 60 miles an hour for the second part. For how many hours did he average 70 miles per hour? (*Hint:* Remember, rate in miles per hour times the time in hours = distance traveled.)

   (A) 1
   (B) 2
   (C) 3
   (D) 4

6. Panita, Bill, and Evan are friends. Panita is six years older than Bill. Evan's age is twice Panita's age. If the sum of their ages is 74, how old is Panita?

   (A) 14
   (B) 20
   (C) 28
   (D) 34

Answers start on page 46.

© New Readers Press. All rights reserved.

Use the Calculator to Solve Algebra Problems

For some questions on the GED Math Test, you will be able to use an on-screen version of the TI-30XS calculator. These calculator keys will be helpful with algebraic expressions:

power
square root
square
parentheses
negative

- To enter a **negative number,** press the negative [(–)] sign and then enter the number.
- Use [(] and [)] to enclose operations in **grouping symbols.**
- To **square** a number, enter the number and then press [x^2].
- To raise a number to some other **power,** enter the number, press [^], and then enter the power.
- To find the **square root** of a number, press [2nd] [x^2], and then enter the number. The $\sqrt{}$ function is located above the x^2 key.

When evaluating an expression on paper, you must remember to follow the **order of operations:** (1) parentheses and grouping symbols, (2) exponents and powers, (3) multiplication or division from left to right, and (4) addition or subtraction from left to right. The TI-30XS calculator is programmed to use the order of operations in a problem with several steps.

Example

What is the value of $-3(x + 15)$ when $x = 4$?

 THINK: *I can use the calculator to evaluate the expression.*

parentheses keys

Press: [(–)] 3 [×] [(] 4 [+] 15 [)] [ENTER] | −57

SOLUTION: The value of the expression is **–57.**

You can also evaluate this expression using paper and pencil. It takes more steps, but you have a record of each step that makes it easier to check your work. Do you use your calculator? Paper and pencil? A combination? Practice with a variety of methods, and use whatever works best for you.

GED Problem

What is the value of the following expression when $x = 9$ and $y = -6$?
$5x^2y + \sqrt{324}$

- (A) 2,412
- (B) 1,206
- (C) 603
- (D) –2,412

 THINK: *I can use a calculator to find the value.*

Step 1: When there are two or more variables, rewrite the expression and substitute the correct values: $5 \times 9^2 \times -6 + \sqrt{324}$

Step 2: Press:
5 × 9 [x^2] × [(–)] 6 + [2nd] [x^2] 324 [ENTER] –2412

ANSWER: (D) –2,412

© New Readers Press. All rights reserved.

> **TESTWISE**
>
> You may find it helpful to use a calculator for only a part of the expression. For instance, in the last example you could first use the calculator to find the square root of 324 and then use paper and pencil to complete the problem.

Directions: Solve the problems below. For problems 1–3, first write an expression by substituting the given values. Then solve. You may use your calculator for all or for part of each problem.

1. What is the value of m^2n when $m = -16$ and $n = 8$?

   (A) −256
   (B) 128
   (C) 1,024
   (D) 2,048

   Expression with numbers: _____

2. What is the value of the expression below when $r = 25$, $s = 10$, and $t = 4$?

   $5r - 3st$

   (A) 5
   (B) 120
   (C) 125
   (D) 240

   Expression with numbers: _____

3. What is the value of $x^2 + (x + 10)$ when x is −4?

   (A) 16
   (B) 22
   (C) 150
   (D) 610

   Expression with numbers: _____

4. What is the value of the expression below when $x = -1$ and $y = -2$?

   $$\dfrac{8xy}{y^2}$$

   (*Calculator Hint:* Use parentheses to group everything above the fraction bar. Evaluate the numerator and then divide.)

   (A) −2
   (B) 0
   (C) 2
   (D) 4

5. Evaluate the expression below when $a = 2$ and $b = 4$.

   $3a^2 + 4b^3$

   (A) 12
   (B) 144
   (C) 268
   (D) 720

6. What is the value of the expression $\sqrt{x + y}$ when $x = 16$ and $y = 9$?

   (*Calculator Hint:* Add first; then find the square root.)

   (A) 2
   (B) 3
   (C) 4
   (D) 5

7. Find the value of the expression below when $p = 3$.

   $(2p + 5) + p^2$

   (A) −20
   (B) −10
   (C) 10
   (D) 20

Answers start on page 46.

© New Readers Press. All rights reserved.

Work Backwards to Solve Problems

Most GED algebra problems can be solved quickly by writing and solving an equation.

However, you can also solve a problem by working backwards from the answer choices. Try each answer choice in the problem situation, and see which one works.

Example

Max is 20 years older than twice Brad's age. The sum of their ages is 110. How old is Brad?

(A) 25
(B) 30
(C) 40
(D) 65

 THINK: *I can work backwards from the answer choices to find the correct answer.*

The correct answer choice is Brad's age. If you multiply Brad's age by 2 and add 20, you should get Max's age. The sum of the ages must be 110.

Option (1): If Brad is 25, then Max is 2(25) + 20 = 70. The sum of 20 and 70 *is not* 110.

Option (2): If Brad is 30, then Max is 2(30) + 20 = 80. The sum of 30 and 80 *is* 110.

It isn't necessary to try the other options.

SOLUTION: The correct option is **(B)** 30.

GED Problem 1

The sum of three consecutive even numbers is 234. What is the first number in the series?

(A) 82
(B) 80
(C) 78
(D) 76

 THINK: *I will start with each answer option and add the next two even numbers until I get a sum of 234.*

Try the answer options:

(A) 82 + 84 + 86 = 252
(B) 80 + 82 + 84 = 246
(C) 78 + 80 + 82 = 240
(D) 76 + 78 + 80 = 234

ANSWER: (D) 76

Hint: You could eliminate the first three options by adding the numbers in the ones place. For example, you could eliminate (1), since 2 + 4 + 6 = 1<u>2</u> and the sum 234 ends in 4.

GED Problem 2

Together, Sara and Jeff earn $990 per week. If Sara earns $130 more per week than Jeff earns, how much does Jeff earn per week?

(A) $410
(B) $420
(C) $430
(D) $450

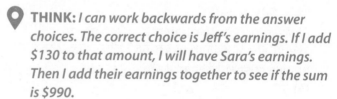 **THINK:** *I can work backwards from the answer choices. The correct choice is Jeff's earnings. If I add $130 to that amount, I will have Sara's earnings. Then I add their earnings together to see if the sum is $990.*

Try the answer options:

(A) $410 + $130 = $540, and $540 + $410 = $950
(B) $420 + $130 = $550, and $550 + $420 = $970
(C) $430 + $130 = $560, and $560 + $430 = $990

ANSWER: (C) $430

© New Readers Press. All rights reserved.

TESTWISE

Try the answer options in the order that makes sense to you. For instance, if some of the choices seem unreasonably high or low, start with a more likely choice.

Directions: Solve the problems below. For problems 1–3, show how you can work backwards from the answer choices.

1. Susan has five bills in both $5 and $10 denominations. If the total value of the bills is $35, how many are $5 bills?

   (A) 1
   (B) 2
   (C) 3
   (D) 4

   Work backwards: _____

2. The length of a rectangular field is 12 yards less than the field's width. If the sum of the length and the width is 96 yards, what is the length of the field in yards?

   (A) 22
   (B) 42
   (C) 54
   (D) 56

   Work backwards: _____

3. The sum of three consecutive odd numbers is 57. Which of the following numbers is the largest number in the series?

   (A) 11
   (B) 17
   (C) 19
   (D) 21

   Work backwards: _____

4. Stacey is three times as old as Seth. If the difference in their ages is 18 years, how old is Seth?

   (A) 9
   (B) 12
   (C) 15
   (D) 18

Problem 5 refers to the following information.

Novelty Trading Company

Item	Price per Dozen
Yo-yo key chains	$14.00
Glitter jump ropes	$12.00
Foam jet gliders	$6.00

5. Maria bought prizes for a fund-raising event from the Novelty Trading Company. She bought the same number of jump ropes as gliders. If she spent $72 in all, how many dozen gliders did she buy?

   (A) 1
   (B) 2
   (C) 4
   (D) 8

6. Lance has two part-time jobs. Last week he earned a total of $488. He earned $50 more at his job as a security guard than he did at his job at the print shop. How much did he earn at the print shop last week?

   (A) $189
   (B) $219
   (C) $244
   (D) $269

Answers start on page 46.

© New Readers Press. All rights reserved.

Problem-Solving Strategies

Part I: You *may* use a calculator. For questions 1–7, choose the one best answer. For question 8, write your answer in the box.

1. What is the value of the following expression when $x = -4$ and $y = -3$?

   $2x^2y + \sqrt{x^2 + y^2}$

   (A) 101
   (B) 11
   (C) –71
   (D) –91

2. Evaluate the expression below when $a = 4$ and $b = 2$.

   $a^2 + 6b^3$

   (A) 28
   (B) 44
   (C) 64
   (D) 388

3. What is the value of the expression below when $x = -25$ and $y = -5$?

   $\dfrac{xy}{y^2}$

   (A) 125
   (B) 25
   (C) 5
   (D) –5

4. What is the value of m^2n when $m = -20$ and $n = -3$?

   (A) –1,200
   (B) –60
   (C) 400
   (D) 1,200

5. Angela has a total of seven nickels and dimes. If the total value of the coins is $0.60, how many coins are nickels?

   (A) 1
   (B) 2
   (C) 3
   (D) 4

6. Roberto drives his delivery route each day. The following expression represents the miles Roberto drives to his first three delivery stops.

   $3x + (x - 10)$

   How many miles does he drive if $x = 22$?

   (A) 66
   (B) 78
   (C) 98
   (D) 102

7. Marie and Rachel's combined weekly pay is $900. The following expression can be used to solve for Rachel's weekly pay.

   $900 - (0.75p + 25)$

   If $p = 600$, what is Rachel's pay?

   (A) $425
   (B) $431
   (C) $655
   (D) $900

8. What is the value of the expression below when $r = 5$, $s = 20$, and $t = 4$?

   $5s - 3rt$

© New Readers Press. All rights reserved.

Part II: You *may not* use a calculator.
For questions 9–13, choose the one best answer.
For question 14, write your answer in the box.

9. The sum of three consecutive even numbers is 138. What is the largest of these numbers?
   (*Hint:* Consecutive even numbers can be shown as $x, x + 2, x + 4$, and so on.)
   (A) 44
   (B) 46
   (C) 48
   (D) 50

10. The sum of three consecutive odd numbers is 75. Which of the following numbers is the lowest number in the series?
    (A) 21
    (B) 23
    (C) 25
    (D) 27

11. Raul sold three times as many raffle tickets as Amy. Amy sold $50 more in tickets than Michael. Together, they sold $700 in raffle tickets. How many dollars worth of raffle tickets did Raul sell?
    (A) $100
    (B) $150
    (C) $300
    (D) $450

12. At a local skating rink, the admission cost is $5 for adults and $3 for children. On Saturday, 110 children skated. If the skating rink took in $550, how many adults skated?
    (A) 44
    (B) 73
    (C) 110
    (D) 220

13. Last week, Ava and John sold $1,225 in merchandise. If John sold three times more than Ava, how many dollar's worth of merchandise did Ava sell?
    (A) $306.25
    (B) $408.33
    (C) $612.50
    (D) $918.75

14. Richard is seven years older than Lilia. In ten years, the sum of their ages will be 51. How old is Richard now?

    [   ] years old

For more practice with answering questions like this on the computer, you can go to onlinepractice.newreaderspress.com.

SCOREBOOST ACTION PLAN

Check your answers starting on page 47. Fill in the chart, and make an action plan.

Results
0–7 correct • *Need to study more—make a plan*
8–11 correct • *Need to review some skills*
12–14 correct • *Mastery of skills—move on*

Questions	Strategy	Pages	Correct/Total	Plan: More work needed
9, 11, 13, 14	Using Tables	26–27	_____ /4	☐
1, 2, 3, 4, 6, 7, 8	Calculator Skills	28–29	_____ /7	☐
5, 10, 12	Working Backwards	30–31	_____ /3	☐
		Total:	_____ /14	

© New Readers Press. All rights reserved.

Plot Points on Coordinate Grids

The **coordinate grid** is a system of lines used to locate points on a plane. Each point has its own address. The address, or **coordinates** of a point, is a pair of numbers. The numbers can be positive, negative, or both. The first number locates the point horizontally along the **x-axis.** The second number shows the point's location in relation to the vertical **y-axis.** On the grid to the right, point A is located at (–4, 2).

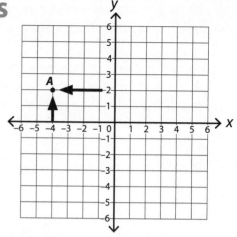

On the GED Math Test, some of the questions will ask you to click on a special coordinate grid to show the location of a point. For practice, you will shade the circle where you would click the grid.

Example

Plot a point with coordinates (5, 3) on the grid.

📍 **THINK:** *The first number shows the location along the x-axis. The second number shows the location along the y-axis.*

Start at the origin (0, 0). On this special GED coordinate grid, the circle marked 0 is the origin. Count five circles to the right along the x-axis. Then count three circles up along the y-axis. Mark your answer on the coordinate plane grid.

SOLUTION: See the grid below.

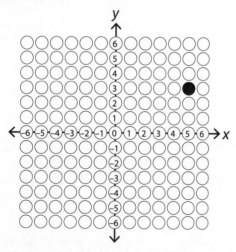

GED Problem

A rectangle is drawn on a coordinate grid. Its vertices, or corners, are located at (–2, –4), (–2, 1), and (4, –4). At what point is the fourth vertex?

Mark your answer on the coordinate plane grid.

📍 **THINK:** *I know a rectangle has four sides, and the opposite sides are equal. I can plot the three points given in the problem, and then determine where the fourth point must be placed.*

First, plot the three points given in the problem.

To form a rectangle, the fourth point must be located at (4, 1). Fill in this circle on the answer grid. The answer is shown below.

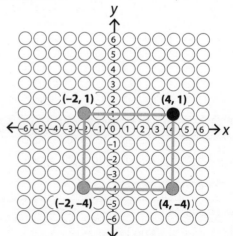

© New Readers Press. All rights reserved.

TESTWISE

To mark a point (x, y) on the GED coordinate grid, start with the x-value and count to the right if the number is positive or to the left if it is negative. Then count the number of places for the y-value: up if it is positive or down if it is negative. Tap the grid carefully. If you need to erase a point, place the arrow over the point and click the left mouse button.

Directions: Solve the problems below. For problems 1 and 2, write the answer first as a coordinate pair. Then mark your answers on the coordinate plane grids.

1. A point has an *x*-coordinate of 3 and a *y*-coordinate of –2. What is the location of the point on the coordinate grid?

   Coordinate pair: _____

   Mark your answer on the blank coordinate grid below.

   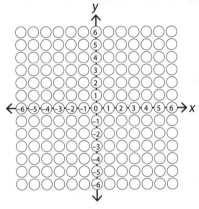

2. The coordinate grid below shows the graph of a circle. What point is located at the center of the circle?

   Coordinate pair: _____

   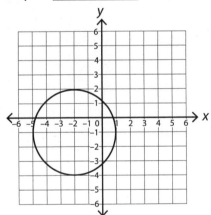

   Mark your answer on the blank coordinate grid below.

   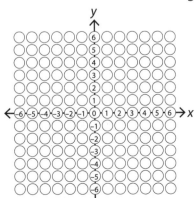

3. A point has an *x*-coordinate of –4 and a *y*-coordinate of –2. What is the location of the point on the coordinate grid?

   Mark your answer on the blank coordinate grid below.

   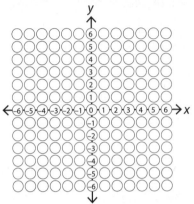

4. The coordinate grid below shows the location of three vertices of a parallelogram. At what point is the fourth vertex?

   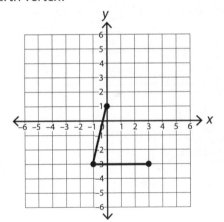

   Mark your answer on the blank coordinate grid below.

   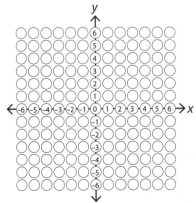

Answers start on page 47.

© New Readers Press. All rights reserved.

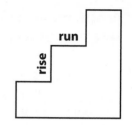

Use the Formula to Find Slope

Slope is a measure of the steepness of a line. To find the slope, write the ratio of the **rise** of the line to the **run.** Think of a flight of stairs. If you were walking up the stairs shown to the right, each step would take you up and forward. The upward movement is the rise, and the forward movement is the run.

On a coordinate grid, slope is said to be **positive** when the line rises as it goes from left to right. The slope is said to be **negative** if the line moves downward as it goes from left to right.

If a line is drawn on a coordinate grid, you can often find the slope easily by counting spaces to find the rise and the run. On the GED test, the slope formula is provided on the Mathematics Formula Sheet. Use whichever method is easier for you.

Example

What is the slope of line *AB* shown on the grid below?

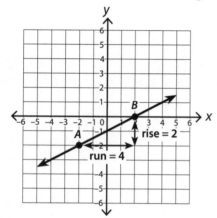

🔘 **THINK:** *I will use points A and B on the line and the formula for slope.*

The formula for slope is $m = \frac{y_2 - y_1}{x_2 - x_1}$. *A* is located at (–2, –2) and *B* is at (2, 0). Substitute the coordinates of *A* for (x_1, y_1) and *B* for (x_2, y_2).

$$m = \frac{y_2 - y_1}{x_2 - x_1} = \frac{0 - (-2)}{2 - (-2)} = \frac{2}{4} = \frac{1}{2}$$

SOLUTION: The slope of line *AB* is $\frac{1}{2}$.

TESTWISE

When an equation is written in the form $y = mx + b$, where *m* is one number and *b* is another, the value for *m* is the slope. *Example:* If you graph the equation $y = -2x + 3$, the slope is –2.

GED Problem

Which of the lines on the coordinate grid below has a slope of –1?

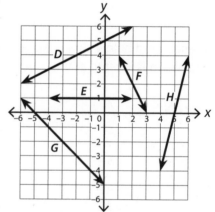

(A) D
(B) E
(C) F
(D) G

🔘 **THINK:** *I can count spaces to find a slope of –1.*

Step 1: Examine each line. A line with a negative slope moves downward from left to right, so we can eliminate lines D, E, and H. Line D and H have a positive slope, and Line E has a slope of 0.

Step 2: Find the slope for lines *F* and *G*. Line *F* goes down two spaces for each one space it runs, for a slope of $-\frac{2}{1}$ or –2. Line *G* goes down one space for each one space it runs, for a slope of $-\frac{1}{1}$ or –1. Line *G* is the correct answer.

ANSWER: (D) G

© New Readers Press. All rights reserved.

**Directions: Find the slope of each line. For questions 1-3, use the graph to identify the ratio of $\frac{rise}{run}$.
Then, find the slope.**

slope of a line $\quad m = \dfrac{y_2 - y_1}{x_2 - x_1}$

Use the following image for questions 1–3.

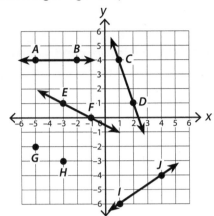

Use the following image for questions 4–6.

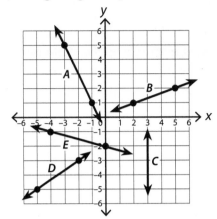

1. line *CD*

    (A) 3

    (B) $\frac{1}{3}$

    (C) $-\frac{1}{3}$

    (D) –3

    $\frac{rise}{run}$: _____

2. line *AB*

    (A) 0

    (B) 1

    (C) 2

    (D) 3

    $\frac{rise}{run}$: _____

3. line *HI*

    (A) $\frac{4}{3}$

    (B) $\frac{3}{4}$

    (C) $-\frac{3}{4}$

    (D) $-\frac{4}{3}$

    $\frac{rise}{run}$: _____

4. Line *A*

    (A) 2

    (B) $\frac{1}{2}$

    (C) $-\frac{1}{2}$

    (D) –2

5. Line *E*

    (A) –4

    (B) $-\frac{1}{4}$

    (C) $\frac{1}{4}$

    (D) 4

6. Which line has a slope of $\frac{2}{3}$?

    (A) *A*

    (B) *B*

    (C) *C*

    (D) *D*

Answers start on page 47.

© New Readers Press. All rights reserved.

Use the Formula to Find the Equation of a Line

Every line has an equation that represents it. There are two forms of this equation that you need to know for the GED test:

slope-intercept form: $y = mx + b$
and
point-slope form: $y - y_1 = m(x - x_1)$

Both forms are on the Mathematics Formula Sheet. In each case, the variables are x and y, and m is the slope. The y-intercept is b; this is the point where the line crosses the y-axis, which is always the point $(0, b)$. The coordinates of a point on the graph are represented by (x_1, y_1).

To write the equation in slope-intercept form:
- If you are given the slope and the y-intercept: write the equation.
- If you are given two points and the y-intercept: find the slope, and then write the equation.
- If you are given two points: find the slope, then substitute the slope and one point for x and y to solve for b. Then, write the equation using m and b.

To write the equation in point-slope form:
- If you are given the slope and a point: write the equation.
- If you are given two points: find the slope, and then use one point and the slope to write the equation.

Example

A line contains the points (1, 5) and (2, 7). Write the equation of the line in slope-intercept form.

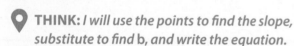 **THINK:** *I will use the points to find the slope, substitute to find b, and write the equation.*

On the GED test, you can refer to the Mathematics Formula Sheet to find the equations.

Step 1: $m = \frac{7 - 5}{2 - 1} = \frac{2}{1} = 2$

Step 2: Substitute 2 for m. Then, substitute the point (1, 5).

$y = mx + b$
$5 = 2(1) + b$
$5 = 2 + b$
$3 = b$

SOLUTION: The equation of the line is **$y = 2x + 3$.**

GED Problem

A line contains the points (2, –3) and (4, –2). What is the equation of this line in point-slope form?

(A) $y - 2 = \frac{1}{2}(x - (-3))$

(B) $y + 3 = \frac{1}{2}(x - 2)$

(C) $y + 2 = 2(x - 4)$

(D) $y - 3 = 2(x + 4)$

THINK: *I need to find the slope and then use one of the points to write the equation.*

Step 1: $m = \frac{-3 - (-2)}{2 - 4} = \frac{-1}{-2} = \frac{1}{2}$

Step 2: I'll use the point (2, –3) to write an equation.

$y - (-3) = \frac{1}{2}(x - 2)$
$y + 3 = \frac{1}{2}(x - 2)$

ANSWER: (B) $y + 3 = \frac{1}{2}(x - 2)$

TESTWISE

An *intercept* is a point on a line. The y-intercept can be written as the point $(0, b)$. The x-intercept can be written as the point $(n, 0)$.

© New Readers Press. All rights reserved.

Directions: Solve the problems below. Find the equation of the line that has the given slope and/or passes through the given points. For questions 1–3, identify the form of the equation for which you are looking.

slope-intercept form of the equation of a line $y = mx + b$
point-slope form of the equation of a line $y - y_1 = m(x - x_1)$

1. $m = \frac{-2}{3}$; (3, 4)

   (A) $y = 4x - \frac{2}{3}$

   (B) $y = 3x + 4$

   (C) $y = -\frac{2}{3}x + 4$

   (D) $y = -\frac{2}{3}x + 6$

   Form: _____

2. $m = -5$; (0, 10)

   (A) $y = -5x + 2$

   (B) $y = -5x + 10$

   (C) $y = -2x + 10$

   (D) $y = -2x - 5$

   Form: _____

3. $m = -\frac{4}{3}$; (2, –1)

   (A) $y + 1 = -\frac{4}{3}(x - 2)$

   (B) $y - 1 = -\frac{4}{3}(x + 2)$

   (C) $x - 2 = -\frac{4}{3}(y + 1)$

   (D) $y + 1 = -\frac{3}{4}(x - 2)$

   Form: _____

4. $m = -\frac{1}{3}$; (9, 0)

   (A) $y = 9x - \frac{1}{3}$

   (B) $y = \frac{1}{3}x - 9$

   (C) $y = -\frac{1}{3}x + 3$

   (D) $y = -\frac{1}{3}x + 9$

5. (3, –1) and (–3, 5)

   (A) $y + 1 = -(x + 3)$

   (B) $y + 5 = -(x - 3)$

   (C) $y - 5 = x + 3$

   (D) $y - 5 = -(x + 3)$

6. $m = 0$; (4, –7)

   (A) $y - 7 = 0$

   (B) $y + 7 = 0$

   (C) $y + 7 = 4x$

   (D) $y + 7 = x - 4$

Answers start on page 47.

© New Readers Press. All rights reserved.

Points, Lines, and Slope on the Coordinate Plane

Part I: You *may* use a calculator.
For questions 1–3, choose the one best answer.
For question 4, write your answer in the box. For question 5, mark your answer on the grid.

slope of a line $m = \dfrac{y_2 - y_1}{x_2 - x_1}$

slope-intercept $y = mx + b$

point-slope $y - y_1 = m(x - x_1)$

1. Point *A* at (–1, –2) and point *B* at (1, 2) lie on the same line. Which of the following is the equation of the line?

   (A) $y = 3x$
   (B) $y = 2x$
   (C) $y = 2x + 2$
   (D) $y = x + 2$

2. What is the slope of line *AB*? (*Hint:* What two points are on line *AB*?)

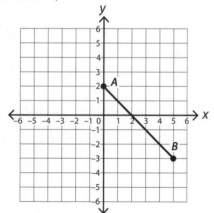

   (A) 5
   (B) 1
   (C) $-\dfrac{1}{5}$
   (D) –1

3. Which equation of a line is graphed below? (*Hint:* Find two points on the line.)

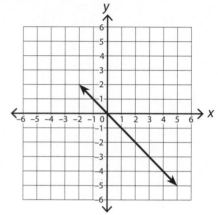

   (A) $y - 3 = -1(x + 3)$
   (B) $y + 1 = -1(x - 3)$
   (C) $y + 3 = -1(x - 3)$
   (D) $y + 1 = -3(x - 1)$

4. A line passes through two points with the coordinates (–2, 1) and (4, 5). What is the slope of this line? Write your answer in the box.

   The slope of the line is [   ].

5. A point has an *x*-coordinate of –4 and a *y*-coordinate of 2. What is the location of the point on the coordinate grid?
   Mark your answer on the coordinate plane grid below.

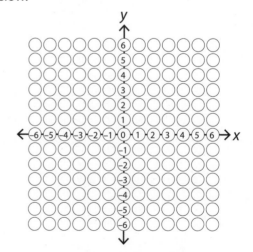

For more practice with answering questions like this on the computer, you can go to **onlinepractice.newreaderspress.com.**

© New Readers Press. All rights reserved.

Part II: You *may not* use a calculator.
For questions 6–8, choose the one best answer. For questions 9 and 10, mark your answer on the grid.

slope of a line $\quad m = \dfrac{y_2 - y_1}{x_2 - x_1}$

slope-intercept $\quad y = mx + b$

point-slope $\quad y - y_1 = m(x - x_1)$

6. The coordinate grid below shows the graph of a circle. What point is located at the center of the circle?

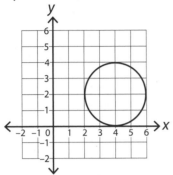

(A) (3, 2)
(B) (5, 2)
(C) (2, 4)
(D) (4, 2)

7. Which equation of a line is graphed below?

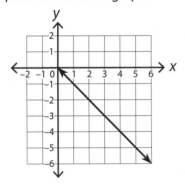

(A) $y = -x$
(B) $y = x - 1$
(C) $y = x + 1$
(D) $y = x - 3$

8. Point *A* at (–1, 1) and point *B* at (1, 3) lie on the same line. Which of the following equations is the equation of the line?

(A) $y = 3x$
(B) $y = 2x + 1$
(C) $y = 2x + 2$
(D) $y = x + 2$

9. The coordinate grid below shows the location of three vertices of a parallelogram. At what point is the fourth vertex?
Mark your answer on the coordinate plane grid below.

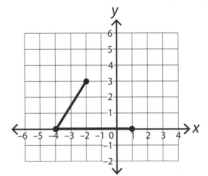

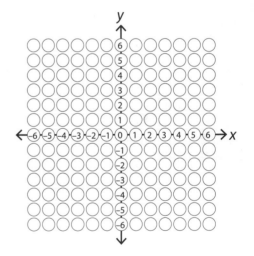

SCOREBOOST ACTION PLAN

Check your answers starting on page 47. Fill in the chart, and make an action plan.

Results
0–5 correct • *Need to study more—make a plan*
6–7 correct • *Need to review some skills*
8–9 correct • *Mastery of skills—move on*

Questions	Strategy	Pages	Correct/Total	Plan: More work needed
5, 6, 9	Points on Coordinate Grids	34–35	_____ /3	☐
2, 4	Slope of a Line	36–37	_____ /2	☐
1, 3, 7, 8	Equation of a Line	38–39	_____ /4	☐
		Total:	_____ /9	

© New Readers Press. All rights reserved.

Part I: You *may* use a calculator.
For questions 1 through 10, choose the one best answer. Write your answer in the box for question 11. Mark your answer on the coordinate plane grid for questions 12 and 13.

quadratic formula $\quad x = \dfrac{-b \pm \sqrt{b^2 - 4ac}}{2a}$

slope of a line $\quad m = \dfrac{y_2 - y_1}{x_2 - x_1}$

slope-intercept $\quad y = mx + b$

point-slope $\quad y - y_1 = m(x - x_1)$

1. What is the value of the expression below when $x = -9$ and $y = 6$?

   $\dfrac{x^2}{x + y}$

   (A) 27
   (B) 6
   (C) −27
   (D) −81

2. Guy has a total of nine $20 bills and $5 bills. If the total value of the bills is $105, how many bills are $5 bills?

   (A) 4
   (B) 5
   (C) 6
   (D) 7

3. What is the value of the following expression when $x = -7$ and $y = 13$?

   $\sqrt{x^2 - y} + xy$

   (A) 97
   (B) 12
   (C) −85
   (D) −91

4. Solve $10 - 2x < 22$

   (A) $x > -6$
   (B) $x > 6$
   (C) $x < -6$
   (D) $x < 6$

5. Solve using the quadratic formula:
   $x^2 + 12x + 10 = -8$

   (A) $x = 10.243, 1.757$
   (B) $x = -1.75, -10.243$
   (C) $x = 9.392, -11.392$
   (D) $x = 11.392, -9.392$

6. Five more than 3 times a number is −22. What is the number?

   (A) $x = -9$
   (B) $x = -5$
   (C) $x = 6$
   (D) $x = 8$

7. What is the slope of line AB?

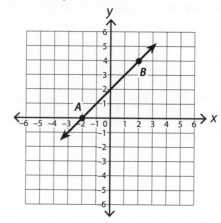

   (A) 4
   (B) 1
   (C) $-\dfrac{1}{4}$
   (D) −1

8. A cartographer creates a map using the function $d = 250n$ where n is the number of inches on the map and d is the actual distance between the locations in miles. If the actual distance between two cities is 1,125 miles, how far apart on the map should the cities be?

   (A) 0.5 inches
   (B) 1.5 inches
   (C) 2.5 inches
   (D) 4.5 inches

9. Point R is located at (3, 0). Point S is located at (0, −4). What is the equation of the line through these two points?

   (A) $y = -\dfrac{3}{4}x + 3$
   (B) $y = -\dfrac{4}{3}x - 4$
   (C) $y = \dfrac{3}{4}x - 3$
   (D) $y = \dfrac{4}{3}x - 4$

© New Readers Press. All rights reserved.

10. What is the value of the expression below when $r = 4$, $s = 5$, and $t = -12$?

    $t^2 - rst$

    (A) -240
    (B) 96
    (C) 384
    (D) $8,800$

11. A rectangle has an area of 168 square inches. The width is 12 inches. Solve the equation to find the length of the rectangle: $168 = x(12)$

    The length of the rectangle is ☐ inches.

12. A point has an x-coordinate of 5 and a y-coordinate of -4. What is the location of the point on the coordinate grid?
    Mark your answer on the coordinate plane grid below.

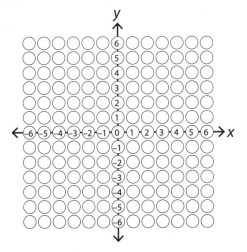

13. Three vertices of a square are $(2, 0)$, $(-3, 0)$, and $(2, 5)$. What is the location of the fourth vertex? Mark your answer on the coordinate plane grid below.

Part II: You *may not* use a calculator.
For questions 14 through 23, choose the one best answer. Write your answer in the box for question 24. Mark your answer on the coordinate plane grid for question 25.

14. The sum of three consecutive even numbers is 96. What is the largest of these numbers?
    (A) 30
    (B) 32
    (C) 34
    (D) 36

15. Solve by factoring. $x^2 - 8x = 33$
    (A) $x = 11, -3$
    (B) $x = 3, 11$
    (C) $x = 3, -11$
    (D) $x = -11, -3$

16. $-4 \cdot -5 \cdot -2$
    (A) -40
    (B) -22
    (C) 18
    (D) 40

17. Teresa and Janet both sold boxes of cookies to raise money for their club. Teresa sold three times as many boxes as Janet. If they sold a total of 80 boxes, how many boxes of cookies did Teresa sell?
    (A) 10
    (B) 20
    (C) 40
    (D) 60

18. $-24 + 16$
    (A) -40
    (B) -8
    (C) 8
    (D) 40

19. $12 - (-2)$
    (A) -14
    (B) -10
    (C) 10
    (D) 14

20. $\dfrac{-32}{-8}$
    (A) -40
    (B) -4
    (C) 4
    (D) 40

© New Readers Press. All rights reserved.

21. The graph below shows the number of customer calls the Info Hotline got during its first eight months of operation. The line approximates the number of calls each month. What is the equation of the line?

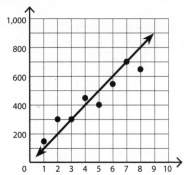

(A) $y - 300 = 1(x - 3)$
(B) $y - 300 = 100(x - 3)$
(C) $y - 100 = 3(x - 1)$
(D) $y + 700 = 100(x + 7)$

22. Which equation of a line is graphed below? (*Hint:* Find two points on the line.)

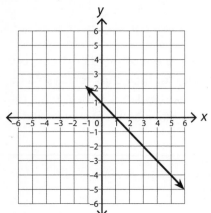

(A) $y = -x$
(B) $y = x - 1$
(C) $y = x + 1$
(D) $y = 1 - x$

23. Point A at (−1, −3) and point B at (2, 6) lie on the same line. Which of the following is the equation of the line?

(A) $y - 6 = 3(x - 2)$
(B) $y - 3 = 3(x - 1)$
(C) $y - 1 = 2(x - 3)$
(D) $y + 3 = 2(x + 1)$

24. Luc is 8 years older than Kate. In 10 years, the sum of their ages will be 88. How old is Luc now?

☐ years old

25. The coordinate grid below shows the location of three vertices of a rectangle. At what point is the fourth vertex?
Mark your answer on the coordinate plane grid below.

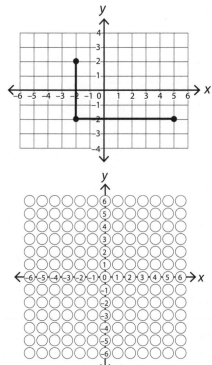

SCOREBOOST ACTION PLAN

Check your answers starting on page 48. Fill in the chart, and make an action plan.

Results
0–13 correct • *Need to study more—make a plan*
14–19 correct • *Need to review some skills*
20–25 correct • *Mastery of skills—move on*

Questions	Strategy	Pages	Correct/Total	Plan: More work needed
1, 3, 10, 16, 18, 19, 20	Integer and Expression Strategies	4–11	_____ /7	☐
4, 5, 6, 8, 11, 15, 17	Equations, Functions, and Inequalities	14–23	_____ /7	☐
2, 14, 22, 24	Problem-Solving Strategies	26–31	_____ /4	☐
7, 9, 12, 13, 21, 23, 25	Points, Lines, and Slope	34–39	_____ /7	☐
		Total:	_____ /25	

© New Readers Press. All rights reserved.

Strategy 1: Add and Subtract Integers, Page 5

1. Addition: $15 + 3$
   (D) 18

2. Addition: $-22 + 9$
   (B) −13

3. Addition: $-24 + (-5)$
   (A) −29

4. **(C) 11**
   $14 + (-3) = 11$

5. **(A) −$40**
   $-23 + (-17) = -40$

6. **(D) 36**
   $14 - (-22) = 14 + 22 = 36$

7. **(A) −26**
   $-4 - 22 = -4 + (-22) = -26$

Strategy 2: Multiply and Divide Integers, Page 7

1. Signs? Same
   (D) 21
   $7(3) = 21$

2. Signs? Different
   (A) −$3,900
   $-325(12) = -3,900$

3. Signs? Different
   (B) −7
   $-42 \div 6 = -7$

4. **(A) −56**
   $4(-14) = -56$

5. **(D) 7**
   $\frac{-56}{-8} = 7$

6. **(D) 60**
   $-12 \cdot -5$

7. **(C) −24**
   $-1 \cdot -2 \cdot -3 \cdot 4 = 2 \cdot -3 \cdot 4 =$
   $-6 \cdot 4 = -24$

Strategy 3: Find Powers and Roots, Page 9

1. Same base? yes
   (C) 243
   $3^2 \cdot 3^3 = 3^5 = 243$

2. Same base? no
   (D) 4
   $\frac{10^2}{5^2} = \frac{100}{25} = 4$

3. Same base? yes
   (B) 8
   $\frac{8^{16}}{8^{15}} = 8^1 = 8$

4. **(D) 256**
   $(2^2)^4$

5. **(D) 9**
   $-3^2 = -3 \times -3 = 9$

6. **(B) 2**
   $\sqrt[5]{32} = 2$, because $2^5 = 32$

7. **(C) 11 and −11**
   $\sqrt{121} = 11, -11$ because
   $11^2 = 121$ and $(-11)^2 = 121$

8. **(A) −4**
   $\sqrt[3]{-64} = -4$ because $(-4)^3 = -64$

Strategy 4: Evaluate Expressions, Page 11

1. Substitution $-x^4 = -1^4$
   (B) −1
   $-x^4 = -1^4 = -1$

2. Substitution:
   $ft - \frac{t}{z} = (-2)(12) - \frac{12}{3}$
   (A) −28
   $ft - \frac{t}{z} = (-2)(12) - \frac{12}{3}$
   $= -24 - 4 = -28$

3. Substitution: $4 - 2x^3 = 4 - 2(3)^3$
   (B) −50
   $4 - 2x^3 = 4 - 2(3)^3 = 4 - 2(27)$
   $= 4 - 54 = -50$

4. **(D) 22**
   $10 - 4d = 10 - 4(-3)$
   $= 10 - (-12) = 22$

5. **(C) −36**
   $2w + 5x = 2(-3) + 5(-6)$
   $= -6 + (-30) = -36$

6. **(C) 18**
   $p + st = -2 + 4(5) = -2 + 20 = 18$

7. **(C) 1**
   $\frac{m+n}{2(m-n)} = \frac{3+1}{2(3-1)} = \frac{4}{2(2)} = \frac{4}{4} = 1$

8. **(B) −96**
   $r(3x + 1) = 12(3(-3) + 1)$
   $= 12(-9 + 1) = 12(-8)$
   $= -96$

Unit 1 Practice, Pages 12–13

1. **(C) $225**
   $340 + (-115) = 225$

2. **(D) 5**
   $\frac{3n+8}{h} = \frac{3(-6)+8}{-2} = \frac{-10}{-2} = 5$

3. **(A) −48**
   $4(-12) = -48$

4. **(A) −$13**
   $\frac{-10 + (-12) + (-17)}{3} = \frac{-39}{3} = -13$

5. **(B) −3**
   $-3 \cdot -3 \cdot -3 = -27$

6. **(A) −8**
   $\frac{-p^2}{q} = \frac{-4^2}{2} = \frac{-16}{2} = -8$

7. **(D) 392**
   $288 - (-104) = 392$

8. **(C) 32**
   $4^3 - 2^5 = 64 - 32 = 32$

9. **(C) 33**
   $4m^2 - 3 = 4(-3)^2 - 3$
   $= 4(9) - 3$
   $= 36 - 3 = 33$

10. **(C) 32**
    $2^2 \cdot 2^3 = 2^5 = 32$

11. **(A) 12 and −12**
    $12 \cdot 12 = 144$
    $-12 \cdot -12 = 144$

12. **(D) 81**
    $(3^2)^2 = 9^2 = 81$

13. **(B) −2**
    $\frac{-2x^2}{z+b} = \frac{-2(-4)^2}{11+5} = \frac{-2(16)}{16} = \frac{-32}{16} = -2$

14. **(C) 13**
    $-26 + 39 = 13$

15. **(D) 36**
    $12 - (-24) = 12 + 24 = 36$

16. **(A) −24**
    $-2 \cdot -3 = 6$
    $6 \cdot -4 = -24$

17. **(B) −4**
    $-32 \div 8 = -4$

Strategy 5: Write and Solve Equations, Page 15

1. Let $x =$ the first day's distance.
   (A) 175 miles
   $x = $ 1st day's distance
   $2x - 100 = $ 2nd day's distance
   $2(2x - 100) = $ 3rd day's distance
   $2(2x - 100) = 500$
   $2x - 100 = 250$
   $2x = 350$
   $x = 175$

2. Let $n =$ the number.
   (B) 4
   $n + 1 = 5n - 15$
   $n + 16 = 5n$
   $16 = 4n$
   $4 = n$

3. Let $p =$ Rita's weekly pay.
   (C) $320
   $p = $ Rita's pay
   $0.5p + 40 = $ Bill's pay
   $p + 0.5p + 40 = 520$
   $1.5p = 480$
   $p = 320$

4. **(D) 20**
   Find the number of red marbles and double it.
   $x + 2x + 2x + 5 = 55$
   $5x = 50$
   $x = 10$
   $2(10) = 20$

5. **(A) 4**
   Let $x = $ Samuel's age now
   Let $4x = $ Maggie's age
   $4x + 5 = 3(x + 5) - 6$
   $4x + 5 = 3x + 15 - 6$
   $4x + 5 = 3x + 9$
   $x = 4$

6. **(D) 22**
   The difference between n and 5 is $n - 5$. The product of -2 and the difference is written $-2(n - 5)$.
   Let $n = $ the first number
   Let $-2(n-5) = $ the second number
   Solve for the first number and use it to solve for the second number.
   $n + (-2)(n - 5) = 16$
   $n - 2n + 10 = 16$
   $-n = 6$
   $n = -6$
   $-2(-6 - 5) = -2(-11) = 22$

Strategy 6: Evaluate Functions, Page 17

1. Function: $d = 56h$
   (D) 1,344 miles
   $d = 56(24) = 1,344$ miles

2. Function: $A = 30 + 12(5) + 2n$
   (C) $252
   $A = 30 + 12(5) + 2(81) = 252$

3. Function: $P = 0.15s$
   (B) $648
   $P = 0.15(4320) = 648$

4. **(C) $6.70**
   $F = 6 + 0.10(n - 10)$
   $= 6 + 0.10(17 - 10)$
   $= 6 + 0.10(7) = 6 + 0.70 = 6.70$

5. **(A) 7**
   In this case, you are given the dependent variable, or the output, and you need to find the input.
   $c = 2y$
   $14 = 2y$
   $7 = y$

6. **(C) 91.44**
   $n = 2.54c$
   $n = 2.54(36)$
   $n = 91.44$

Strategy 7: Solve Inequalities, Page 19

1. Inequality: $50 + 65d \le 850$
   (D) $d \le 12$
   $50 + 65d \le 850$
   $65d \le 800$
   $d \le 12.3$
   She cannot pay for a partial month, so the solution is $d \le 12$.

2. Inequality: $900 \ge 76m$
   (A) $m \le 11$
   $\frac{900}{76} \ge \frac{76m}{76}$
   $11.8 \ge m$
   She cannot make it an entire 12 months, so the number is rounded down.

3. Inequality: $.07s \ge 400$
   (C) $s \ge $5,714.29$
   $\frac{0.07s}{0.07} \ge \frac{400}{0.07}$
   $s \ge 5,714.29$

4. **(B) $m \le 325$**
   If she drives 65 mph the entire 5 hours, she could go 325 miles, so the inequality is less than or equal to.

5. **(B) $j \ge 7$**
   $j + j + 4 \ge 18$
   $2j + 4 \ge 18$
   $2j \ge 14$
   $j \ge 7$

6. **(A) $t \ge 35$**
   $t + 25 \ge 60$
   $t \ge 35$

Strategy 8: Use FOIL with Quadratic Equations, Page 21

1. Coefficients: $a = 1, b = -6, c = -1$
   (B) $n = 6.162, -0.162$
   $n = \frac{-b \pm \sqrt{b^2 - 4ac}}{2a}$
   $n = \frac{6 \pm \sqrt{(-6)^2 - 4(1)(-1)}}{2(1)}$
   $n = \frac{6 \pm \sqrt{40}}{2}$
   $n = \frac{6 \pm 2\sqrt{10}}{2}$
   $n = 6.162, -0.162$

2. Coefficients: $a = 2, b = -3, c = -5$
   (C) $p = -1, \frac{5}{2}$
   $p = \frac{-b \pm \sqrt{b^2 - 4ac}}{2a}$
   $p = \frac{3 \pm \sqrt{(-3)^2 - 4(2)(-5)}}{2(2)}$
   $p = \frac{3 \pm \sqrt{49}}{4}$
   $p = \frac{3 \pm 7}{4}$
   $p = 2.5, -1$

© New Readers Press. All rights reserved.

3. Coefficients: $a = 1$, $b = 3$, $c = -10$
   (C) $r = 2, -5$
   Set one side of the equation to 0:
   $r^2 + 3r - 10 = 0$
   $r = \dfrac{-b \pm \sqrt{b^2 - 4ac}}{2a}$
   $r = \dfrac{-3 \pm \sqrt{3^2 - 4(1)(-10)}}{2(1)}$
   $r = \dfrac{-3 \pm \sqrt{9 - (-40)}}{2}$
   $r = \dfrac{-3 \pm \sqrt{49}}{2}$
   $r = \dfrac{-3 \pm 7}{2}$, or 2 and -5

4. Factors: $(k - 2)(k + 8)$
   (D) $k = 2, -8$

5. Factors: $(d + 5)(d + 11)$
   (A) $d = -5, -11$

6. Factors: $(y - 2)(y - 5)$
   (D) $y = 2, 5$

Strategy 9: Fill-in-the-Blank Equations and Inequality Questions, Page 23

1. Let x = the width of a tennis court
   Answer: 27
   $3x - 3 = 78$
   $3x = 81$
   $x = 27$

2. Let x = the first number
   Answer: –6
   $x + (-3x) = -4$
   $-2x = -4$
   $x = 2$
   $-3(2) = -6$

3. Let x = how much Frank earns
   Answer: 46
   $x + 10 \leq 56$
   $x \leq 46$

4. Let x = the number of old stamps
   Answer: 49
   $x + 4x - 11 = 64$
   $5x - 11 = 64$
   $5x = 75$
   $x = 15$
   New stamps = $4x - 11 =$
   $4(15) - 11 = 49$

5. Let x = Brian's age
   Answer: 25
   $x + 2x + 5 = 35$
   $3x + 5 = 35$
   $3x = 30$
   $x = 10$
   $2(10) + 5 = 25$

6. Let x = the number of minutes of advertisements
   Answer: 22
   $x + 2x + 6 = 30$
   $3x + 6 = 30$
   $3x = 24$
   $x = 8$

7. **Answer: –7**
   $-4x + 6 \leq 34$
   $-4x \leq 28$
   $x \geq -7$

8. **Answer: 4**
   $-30 = -9x + 6$
   $-36 = -9x$
   $4 = x$

9. **Answer: 14**
   $-44 = -3x - 2$
   $-42 = -3x$
   $14 = x$

10. **Answer: 16**
    $\dfrac{3}{4}x > 12$
    $3x > 48$
    $x > 16$

Unit 2 Practice, Pages 24–25

1. **(C) $x = -0.916, 10.916$**
   $x = \dfrac{-b \pm \sqrt{b^2 - 4ac}}{2a}$
   $x = \dfrac{10 \pm \sqrt{(-10)^2 - 4(1)(-10)}}{2(1)}$
   $x = \dfrac{10 \pm \sqrt{140}}{2}$
   $x = \dfrac{10 \pm 2\sqrt{35}}{2}$
   $x = -0.916, 10.916$

2. **(A) $x \geq -5$**
   $-4x + 9 \leq 29$
   $-4x \leq 20$
   $x \geq -5$

3. **(C) 157.5**
   $d = 45h$
   $d = 45(3.5)$
   $d = 157.5$

4. **(D) \$420**
   $p = 60y$
   $p = 60(7)$
   $p = 420$

5. **Answer: 40**
   $90 = c + 2c + c + 10$
   $90 = 4c + 10$
   $80 = 4c$
   $20 = c$
   $2(20) = 40$

6. **Answer: 15**
   $3w + w - 4 = 16$
   $4w - 4 = 16$
   $4w = 20$
   $w = 5$
   $3(5) = 15$

7. **(D) $x = -2, -3$**
   $x^2 + 5x + 6 = 0$
   $(x + 2)(x + 3) = 0$
   $x = -2, -3$

8. **(A) $x > -5$**
   $3x - 7 > -22$
   $3x > -15$
   $x > -5$

9. **(A) 7 meters**
   $P = 4s$
   $28 = 4s$
   $7 = s$

10. **(B) $x = -6, 2$**
    $x^2 + 4x - 2 = 10$
    $x^2 + 4x - 12 = 0$
    $(x + 6)(x - 2) = 0$
    $x = -6, 2$

11. **Answer: 17**
    $22x \geq 360$
    $x > 16.36$
    16 weeks will not be long enough, so he must save at least 17 weeks to have enough money for the wakeboard.

12. **Answer: 63**
    $x + 5x + 8 = 74$
    $6x + 8 = 74$
    $6x = 66$
    $x = 11$
    $5(11) + 8 = 55 + 8 = 63$

Strategy 10: Use Tables to Solve Algebra Problems, Page 27

1. **(A) 20**

	David's Age	Carrie's Age
Now	x	$3x$
In 5 years	$x + 5$	$3x + 5$

   Write an equation that represents Carrie's age in five years as equal to twice David's age in five years.
   $3x + 5 = 2(x + 5)$
   $3x + 5 = 2x + 10$
   $x = 5$
   Carrie's age in 5 years:
   $3x + 5 = 3(5) + 5 = 20$

2. **(C) 59**

1st Number	2nd Number	3rd Number	4th Number
x	$x + 1$	$x + 2$	$x + 3$

   $x + (x + 1) + (x + 2) + (x + 3) = 230$
   $4x + 6 = 230$
   $4x = 224$
   $x = 56$
   The largest number:
   $x + 3 = 56 + 3 = 59$

3. **(C) \$880**

Alex	Omar	Donna
x	$x + 200$	$2(x + 200)$

   $2(x + 200) + x + 200 + x = 3320$
   $2x + 400 + x + 200 + x = 3320$
   $4x + 600 = 3320$
   $4x = 2720$
   $x = 680$
   Omar earns $x + 200 =$
   $680 + 200 = \$880$

4. **(D) 225**

	Children	Adults
Number of tickets	x	$3x$
Prices	\$4	\$6

   $x + 3x = 300$
   $4x = 300$
   $x = 75$
   The number of adult tickets is $3x = 3 \times 75 = 225$ tickets. You do not need to use the prices to answer the question.

5. **(B) 2**

	First Part	Second Part
Time	x	$6 - x$
Rate × Time	$70x$	$60(6 - x)$

   Let x = the number of hours at 70 mph and $6 - x$ = number of hours at 60 mph. Multiply each time by the rate. The sum of these amounts is the total distance:
   $70x + 60(6 - x) = 380$
   $70x + 360 - 60x = 380$
   $10x + 360 = 380$
   $10x = 20$
   $x = 2$

6. **(B) 20**

Bill	Panita	Evan
x	$6 + x$	$2(6 + x)$

   Let Bill's age = x, Panita's age = $6 + x$, and Evan's age = $2(6 + x)$.
   $x + (6 + x) + 2(6 + x) = 74$
   $4x + 18 = 74$
   $4x = 56$
   $x = 14$
   Panita's age: $6 + x = 6 + 14 = 20$

Strategy 11: Use the Calculator to Solve Algebra Problems, Page 29

You may have used your calculator for all or part of each solution. If you chose to do all or some of the work with pencil and paper, the individual steps are shown.

1. Expression with numbers:
   $m^2 n = (-16)^2 \times 8$
   Answer: (D) 2,048
   Calculator: [(–)]16 [x^2] × 8 [ENTER] 2048
   Solution: $(-16)^2 \times 8 = 256 \times 8 = 2048$

2. Expression with numbers:
   $5r - 3st = 5 \times 25 - 3 \times 10 \times 4$
   Answer: (A) 5
   Calculator: $5 \times 25 - 3 \times 10 \times 4$ [ENTER] 5
   Solution:
   $(5 \times 25) - (3 \times 10 \times 4) = 125 - 120 = 5$

3. Expression with numbers:
   $x^2 + (x + 10) = (-4)^2 + (-4 + 10)$
   Answer: (B) 22
   Calculator:
   [(] [(–)] 4 [)] [x^2] + [(] [(–)] 4 + 10 [)] [ENTER] 22
   Solution: $(-4)^2 + (-4 + 10) = 16 + 6 = 22$

4. **(D) 4**
   Calculator:
   $8 \times$ [(–)] 1 × [(–)] 2 ÷ [(] [(–)] 2 [)] [x^2] [ENTER] 4
   Solution:
   $\dfrac{8xy}{y^2} = \dfrac{8 \times -1 \times -2}{(-2)^2} = \dfrac{16}{4} = 4$

5. **(C) 268**
   Calculator:
   3×2 [x^2] + 4×4 [^] 3 ▶ [ENTER] 268
   Solution: $3a^2 + 4b^3 =$
   $(3 \times 2^2) + (4 \times 4^3) =$
   $(3 \times 4) + (4 \times 64) = 12 + 256 = 268$

6. **(D) 5**
   Calculator: [2nd] [x^2] [(] 16 + 9 [)] [ENTER] 5
   Solution:
   $\sqrt{x + y} = \sqrt{16 + 9} = \sqrt{25} = 5$

7. **(D) 20**
   Calculator:
   $2 \times 3 + 5 + 3$ [x^2] [ENTER] 20
   Solution: $(2p + 5) + p^2 =$
   $(2 \times 3 + 5) + 3^2 = 11 + 9 = 20$

© New Readers Press. All rights reserved.

© New Readers Press. All rights reserved.

Strategy 12: Work Backwards to Solve Problems, Page 31

1. Work backwards: Multiply each answer choice by $5. Test to see which result could be subtracted from $35 to allow for five bills.

   Answer: (C) 3

   Three $5 bills is $15. $35 − $15 = $20. $20 divided by $10 is equal to two bills. Three bills plus two bills is five bills.

2. Work backwards: Subtract each answer choice from 96. Then subtract 12. If the result equals the answer choice, you have the right answer.

   Answer: (B) 42

   96 − 42 − 12 = 42

3. Work backwards: Think of the two odd numbers that come before each answer choice. Add all three odd numbers and see whether the sum is 57.

   Answer: (D) 21

   17 + 19 + 21 = 57

4. **(A) 9**

   If Seth is 9, then Stacey is 3 times 9, which equals 27. 27 − 9 = 18

5. **(C) 4**

   Try each of the answer choices. Only $4 \times \$12 + 4 \times \$6$ equals $72, so Maria bought four dozen gliders.

6. **(B) $219**

   Try each of the answer choices: $219 + $50 = $269, and $269 + $219 = $488

Unit 3 Practice, Pages 32–33

1. **(D) −91**

   Substitute the values in the expression.

   $2(-4)^2(-3) + \sqrt{(-4)^2 + (-3)^2} =$

   $2(16)(-3) + \sqrt{16 + 9} =$

   $-96 + \sqrt{25} = -96 + 5 = -91$

2. **(C) 64**

   Substitute the values and evaluate.

   $4^2 + 6(2^3) = 16 + 6(8) = 16 + 48 = 64$

3. **(C) 5**

   After substituting the values, evaluate above and below the fraction bar first. Then divide.

   $\frac{xy}{y^2} = \frac{-25(-5)}{(-5)^2} = \frac{125}{25} = 5$

4. **(A) −1,200**

   Substitute the values.

   $m^2 n = (-20)^2(-3) = 400(-3) = -1200$

5. **(B) 2**

   Work backwards, using the answer choices. If option (A) were true, Angela would have 1 nickel and 6 dimes, which equals $0.65. Option (A) is incorrect. Using option (B), 2 nickels and 5 dimes would total $0.10 + $0.50 = $0.60. Option (B) is correct.

6. **(B) 78**

   When $x = 22$, the distance he drives is 3(22) + (22 − 10) = 66 + 12 = 78 miles.

7. **(A) $425**

   900 − (0.75 × 600 + 25) =
   900 − (450 + 25) = 900 − 475 = 425

8. **40**

   Substitute the values, and evaluate the expression.

   $5s - 3rt = 5(20) - 3(5)(4) =$
   $100 - 60 = 40$

9. **(C) 48**

   You could create a table.

x	$x + 2$	$x + 4$
44	46	48

   $x + x + 2 + x + 4 = 138$
   $3x + 6 = 138$
   $3x = 132$
   $x = 44$

   Fill in the table. The question asks for the largest of the numbers: $x + 4 = 48$.

10. **(B) 23**

    Work backwards from the answer choices. Starting with option (1), if 21 were the smallest of three consecutive odd numbers, the sum would be 21 + 23 + 25 = 69. This is incorrect. Using option (B): 23 + 25 + 27 = 75. This is the correct option.

11. **(D) $450**

    You could use a table to solve the problem.

    Let x = the amount Michael sold.

Michael	Amy	Raul
x	$x + \$50$	$3(x + \$50)$

    Set up an equation and solve for x.

    $x + x + \$50 + 3(x + \$50) = \$700$
    $2x + \$50 + 3x + \$150 = \$700$
    $5x + \$200 = \$700$
    $5x = \$500$
    $x = \$100$

    The question asks how many dollars worth of tickets Raul sold. Substitute the value for x in $3(x + \$50)$.

    $3(\$100 + \$50) = 3(\$150) = \$450$

12. **(A) 44**

    Since 110 children skated, the rink made $3 × 110 = $330 from the children's tickets.

    $550 − $330 = $220 ÷ 5 = 44 adults

13. **(A) $306.25**

    Let x = amount Ava sold and $3x$ = amount John sold.

    $x + 3x = \$1225$, and $4x = \$1225$, and $x = \$306.25$, which equals the amount Ava sold.

14. **19**

    Use a table to solve the problem.

    Let x = Lilia's age, and $x + 7$ = Richard's age.

Lilia's age in 10 years	Richard's age in 10 years
$x + 10$	$x + 7 + 10$

    Set up an equation using the sum of their ages in 10 years.

    $x + 10 + x + 7 + 10 = 51$
    $2x + 27 = 51$
    $2x = 24$
    $x = 12$

    The question asks how old Richard is now. Substitute the value for x in $x + 7$.

    $12 + 7 = 19$

Strategy 13: Plots Points on Coordinate Grids, Page 35

1. **Coordinate pair: (3, −2)**

2. **Coordinate pair: (−2, −1)**

   The diameter of the circle is six units. Start from the point where the circle touches a vertical and horizontal line on the grid. Count in three units from the side and top or bottom to find the center.

3. **Coordinate pair: (−4, −2)**

4. **Coordinate pair: (4, 1)**

   Opposite sides of a parallelogram are equal, so the missing side must be four units long. Four units to the right of point (0, 1) is (4, 1).

Strategy 14: Use the Formula to Find Slope, Page 37

1. Ratio: $-\frac{3}{1}$

   Answer: (D) −3

   Line CD has a rise of 3 units and a run of 1 unit. Since the line goes down, the slope is negative. Use the points C (1, 4) and D (2, 1) and the formula chart:

   $m = \frac{y_2 - y_1}{x_2 - x_1} = \frac{4 - 1}{1 - 2} = \frac{3}{-1} = -3$

2. Ratio: $\frac{0}{-3}$

   Answer: (A) 0

   Look at points A and B. There is no rise in the line. The run from point A to point B is 3. All horizontal lines have a slope of 0. Use the points A (−5, 4) and B (−2, 4) and the formula chart:

   $m = \frac{y_2 - y_1}{x_2 - x_1} = \frac{4 - 4}{-5 - (-2)} = \frac{0}{-3} = 0$

3. Ratio: $-\frac{3}{4}$

   Answer: (C) $-\frac{3}{4}$

   To connect points H and I, go down three units and then go to the right four units. Since the line slopes downward from left to right, the slope is negative. Use the points H (−3, −3) and I (1, −6) and the formula chart:

   $m = \frac{y_2 - y_1}{x_2 - x_1} = \frac{-3 - (-6)}{-3 - 1} = -\frac{3}{4}$

4. **(D) −2**

   Use the slope formula. (−3, 5) and (−1, 1)

   $m = \frac{y_2 - y_1}{x_2 - x_1} = \frac{1 - 5}{-1 - (-3)} = \frac{-4}{2} = -2$

5. **(B) $-\frac{1}{4}$**

   Line E has a rise of 1 and a run of 4. Since the line slopes downward from left to right, the slope is negative: $-\frac{1}{4}$.

Use any two points on line E (−4, −1) and I (0, −2) and the formula chart:

$m = \frac{y_2 - y_1}{x_2 - x_1} = \frac{-1 - (-2)}{-4 - 0} = -\frac{1}{4}$

6. **(D) D**

   Only lines D and B have a positive slope. Line D has a rise of 2 and a run of 3.

Strategy 15: Use the Formula to Find the Equation of a Line, Page 39

1. slope-intercept form

   Answer: (D) $y = -\frac{2}{3}x + 6$

   Substitute the point and slope into the form, and solve for b.

   $y = mx + b$
   $4 = -\frac{2}{3}(3) + b$
   $4 = -2 + b$
   $6 = b$
   $y = -\frac{2}{3}x + 6$

2. Form: slope-intercept form

   Answer: (B) $y = -5x + 10$

   The slope is −5. (0,10) is the y-intercept. So, $b = 10$.

3. Form: point-slope form

   Answer: (A) $y + 1 = -\frac{4}{3}(x - 2)$

   Use the given slope and point to write the equation.

   $y - y_1 = -\frac{4}{3}(x - x_1)$
   $y - (-1) = -\frac{4}{3}(x - 2)$
   $y + 1 = -\frac{4}{3}(x - 2)$

4. **(C) $y = -\frac{1}{3}x + 3$**

   $y = mx + b$
   $0 = -\frac{1}{3}(9) + b$
   $0 = -3 + b$
   $3 = b$

5. **(D) $y - 5 = -(x + 3)$**

   $m = \frac{5 - (-1)}{-3 - (3)} = \frac{6}{-6} = -1$
   $y - 5 = -1(x + 3)$
   $y - 5 = -(x + 3)$

6. **(B) $y + 7 = 0$**

   $y + 7 = 0(x - 4)$
   $y + 7 = 0$

Unit 4 Practice, Pages 40–41

1. **(B) $y = 2x$**

   Find the slope, and then substitute a point and slope into the formula to get b.

   $m = \frac{y_2 - y_1}{x_2 - x_1} = \frac{(-2 - 2)}{(-1 - 1)} = \frac{-4}{-2} = 2$
   $y = mx + b$
   $2 = 2(1) + b$
   $2 = 2 + b$
   $0 = b$

2. **(D) −1**

   Either count the units of rise over run, or use the formula for finding the slope of a line.

   $\frac{y_2 - y_1}{x_2 - x_1} = \frac{(-3 - 2)}{(5 - 0)} = \frac{-5}{5} = -1$

3. **(C) $y + 3 = -1(x - 3)$**

   Use two points from the line: (1, −1) and (3, −3).

   $m = \frac{y_2 - y_1}{x_2 - x_1} = \frac{(-3 - (-1))}{3 - 1} = \frac{-2}{2} = -1$

Use one point and the slope to write the equation.

$y + 3 = -1(x - 3)$

4. $\frac{2}{3}$

Use the formula for finding the slope of a line.

$$\frac{y_2 - y_1}{x_2 - x_1} = \frac{(1 - 5)}{(-2 - 4)} = \frac{-4}{-6} = \frac{2}{3}$$

5. **(–4, 2)**

You should have plotted a point that is four units to the left on the x-axis (horizontal) and two units up on the y-axis (vertical).

6. **(D) (4, 2)**

The longest distance across a circle is from one edge of the circle to the other edge through the center. This is the diameter. The center of the circle would be located at half this distance. The center of this circle is at (4, 2).

7. **(A) $y = -x$**

Pick at least two points that the line passes through. Use the formula chart to find the slope. Then substitute to find b. Write the equation.

$m = \frac{-1 - (-2)}{1 - 2} = \frac{1}{-1} = -1$

$y = mx + b$

$1 = -1(-1) + b$

$1 = 1 + b$

$0 = b$

8. **(D) $y = x + 2$**

Use the formula chart to find the slope and the equation.

$m = \frac{3 - 1}{1 - (-1)} = \frac{2}{2} = 1$

$y = mx + b$

$1 = 1(-1) + b$

$1 = -1 + b$

$2 = b$

9. **(3, 3)**

A parallelogram has pairs of opposite sides that are parallel and equal in length. To complete this parallelogram, plot a point that makes a side equal in length to the base of the figure (count the units: 5). The point should also have the same y-coordinate as (–2, 3). Five units to the right of (–2, 3) is (3, 3).

GED Test Practice, Pages 42–44

1. **(C) –27**

Substitute the values and evaluate.

$\frac{x^2}{x + y} = \frac{(-9)^2}{-9 + 6} = \frac{81}{-3} = -27$

2. **(B) 5**

One strategy is to work backwards from the answer choices. Option (A) would be four $5 bills ($20) and five $20 bills ($100) for a total of $120. Option (B) would be five $5 bills ($25) and four $20 bills ($80) for a total of $105.

3. **(C) –85**

Evaluate the expressions using the given values.

$\sqrt{x^2 - y} + xy =$

$\sqrt{(-7)^2 - 13} + (-7)(13) = \sqrt{49 - 13}$

$- 91 =$

$\sqrt{36} - 91 =$

$6 - 91 = -85$

4. **(A) $x > -6$**

$10 - 2x < 22$

$-2x < 12$

$x > -6$

5. **(B) $x = -1.75, -10.243$**

$x = \frac{-b \pm \sqrt{b^2 - 4ac}}{2a}$

$x = \frac{-12 \pm \sqrt{12^2 - 4(1)(18)}}{2(1)}$

$x = \frac{-12 \pm \sqrt{72}}{2}$

$x = \frac{-12 \pm 6\sqrt{2}}{2}$

$x = -1.75, -10.243$

6. **(A) –9**

$-22 = 3x + 5$

$-27 = 3x$

$-9 = x$

7. **(B) 1**

Use the slope formula:

$\frac{y_2 - y_1}{x_2 - x_1} = \frac{0 - 4}{-2 - 2} = \frac{-4}{-4} = 1$

8. **(D) 4.5 inches**

Evaluate the function.

$d = 250n$

$1125 = 250n$

$4.5 = n$

9. **(D) $y = \frac{4}{3}x - 4$**

$m = \frac{-4 - 0}{0 - 3} = \frac{-4}{-3} = \frac{4}{3}$

The y-intercept is –4.

10. **(C) 384**

Evaluate the expression.

$t^2 - rst = (-12)^2 - (4)(5)(-12)$

$= 144 + 240 = 384$

11. **14**

Evaluate the function.

$\frac{168}{12} = \frac{x(12)}{12}$

$14 = x$

12. **(5, –4)**

Plot the point on the coordinate grid. First locate the x-coordinate (5), which is five units to the right of the origin. Since the y-coordinate is –4, the point is four units down.

13. **(–3, 5)**

Plot the point on the coordinate grid. First locate the x-coordinate (–3), which is three units to the left of the origin. Since the y-coordinate is 5, the point is five units up.

14. **(C) 34**

You could use a table to organize the information.

x	x + 2	x + 4
30	32	34

$x + x + 2 + x + 4 = 96$

$3x + 6 = 96$

$3x = 90$

$x = 30$

Fill in the chart using this information. The largest of the values is $x + 4 = 34$.

15. **(A) $x = 11, –3$**

$x^2 - 8x = 33$

$x^2 - 8x - 33 = 0$

$(x - 11)(x + 3) = 0$

$x = 11, –3$

16. **(A) –40**

$-4 \cdot -5 \cdot -2 = 20 \cdot -2 = -40$

17. **(D) 60**

Let x = the number of boxes Janet sold. Let $3x$ = the number of boxes Teresa sold.

$x + 3x = 80$

$4x = 80$

$x = 20$ and $3x = 3(20) = 60$

18. **(B) –8**

$-24 + 16 = -8$

19. **(D) 14**

$12 - (-2) = 12 + 2 = 14$

20. **(C) 4**

$\frac{-32}{-8} = 4$

21. **(B) $y - 300 = 100(x - 3)$**

$m = \frac{700 - 300}{7 - 3} = \frac{400}{4} = 100$

Use the point (3, 300) to write the equation in point-slope form.

22. **(D) $y = 1 - x$**

Two points are (0, 1) and (1, 0), and the y-intercept is 1.

$m = \frac{1 - 0}{0 - 1} = \frac{1}{-1} = -1$

23. **(A) $y - 6 = 3(x - 2)$**

First, find the slope.

$m = \frac{6 - (-3)}{2 - (-1)} = \frac{9}{3} = 3$

$y - 6 = 3(x - 2)$

24. **38**

Set up a table to organize the information.

	Now	In 10 years
Kate	x	x + 10
Luc	x + 8	x + 8 +10

Write an equation and solve.

$x + 10 + x + 8 + 10 = 88$

$2x + 28 = 88$

$2x = 60$

$x = 30$

Find out how old Luc is now:

$x + 8 = 30 + 8 = 38$.

25. **(5, 2)**

A rectangle has equal opposite sides. The fourth vertex needs to be directly across from coordinates (–2, 2) and directly up from coordinates (5, –2).

ITEM #2465

Scoreboost FOR THE GED® TEST
Writing Across the Tests | Sentence Structure, Usage, and Mechanics

Scoreboost FOR THE GED® TEST
Writing Across the Tests | Responding to Text on the Language Arts and Science Tests

Scoreboost FOR THE GED® TEST
Mathematics | Fractions, Decimals, Percents, and Proportions

Scoreboost FOR THE GED® TEST
Mathematics | Measurement and Geometry

Scoreboost FOR THE GED® TEST
Mathematics | Graphs, Data Analysis, and Probability

Scoreboost FOR THE GED® TEST
Mathematics | Algebraic Reasoning

Scoreboost FOR THE GED® TEST
Thinking Skills | Critical Thinking for Reading, Science, and Social S

Scoreboost FOR THE GED® TEST
Thinking Skills | Data and Graphic Skills for Mathematics, Science Social Studies

New Readers Press
ProLiteracy's publishing division

Syracuse, New York
800.448.8878
www.newreaderspress.com

ISBN 978-1-56420-465-3

9 781564 204653

T4-BCD-475